An Old-Fashioned Pittsburgh Romance

An Old-Fashioned Pittsburgh Romance

By

Margaret Frances Soboslay

Edited by
Francine M. Costello

ISBN: 1-59571-115-5
Library of Congress Control Number: 2006921654

Word Association Publishers
205 5th Avenue
Tarentum, PA 15084
www.wordassociation.com

This book was written for my daughers
Marie, Ruth, Betsy, Susan, Patricia, Michelle, and their families,
and dedicated to the memory of my parents and grandparents.

Forward

An Old-Fashioned Pittsburgh Romance, began in Pittsburgh in 1934, and moved on to a Central Pennsylvania forest, where strong, able-bodied young men cleared undergrowth, planted trees, built bridges and roads, while strengthening their bodies and minds, and writing impassioned letters home to the ones they love. This all took place in the time of the Great Depression, when people were struggling to put food on their tables, pay the rent, and just keep going.

The city of Pittsburgh was smoky and grimy. Cars mingled with horses and buggies. The banks of the Allegheny River were muddy and littered with abandoned cars. Riverboats, rafts, and coal barges slowly passed as captains saluted each other while on their way to and from the Great Ohio River.

Maggie Rossi was young, brown-haired, blue-eyed, and petite, with a beautiful, beguiling smile. She captured the heart and passions of a younger man. This younger man, Dave Bell, was soon to go two hundred miles away to work in the Civilian Conservation Corps, on Bald Eagle Mountain—far away from Maggie, the girl he loved. He had to find a way to tell her he loved her. The problem was, he had just met her, and didn't want to scare her away. Besides, he was shy, and not very good at putting his feelings into words. It was a problem, but he was bound and determined to get up the courage to tell her just how he felt

before he went away.

Maggie and Dave lived only two blocks from each other, yet were worlds apart in temperament and upbringing. Dave, eighteen, lived quietly with his mom. Maggie, who was twenty, lived in a noisy, happy household, steeped in Italian-Catholic traditions, with protective parents, six sisters, and two brothers.

An *Old Fashioned Pittsburgh Romance* will bring readers back to the time when many young people in Pittsburgh were first-generation Americans. When good jobs were hard to come-by and a romantic evening out meant taking a walk to get an Isaly's ice cream cone. This love story spans forty-five years and illustrates that true love never dies.

Franklin Delano Roosevelt, newly elected President of the United States in 1933, instituted the New Deal, and with it, the Civilian Conservation Corps. The CCC, as it was popularly known, put young men to work in the forests to preserve and restore them, while at the same time providing a means of income for the unemployed. The pay was only thirty dollars a month. But thirty dollars a month at that time was a great deal of money. By August of 1935, the number of men benefiting from the CCC program totaled six hundred thousand.

Part One

Chapter 1
An Old-Fashioned Romance

*D*ave Bell wanted to make things easier for his mother and himself. After a little consideration, he made the decision to join the Civilian Conservation Corps. It was spring and the weather was fair and mild. East Ohio Street, the business district where the recruitment office for the CCC was located, was always bustling. Dave had just signed up and was on his way home to Lovett Way, one of the many narrow streets that ran through the North Side of Pittsburgh.

As he walked, he was startled to see the most beautiful girl in the world coming toward him. He'd seen her from a distance a few times before but never this close.

The sidewalk was narrow. As he passed her, trying not to stare, he jostled her arm, and she almost dropped the books she was returning to the North Side branch of the Carnegie Library. The pink rose she had on top of them slid off and into Dave's path. As he bent to retrieve it at the same time she did, they bumped heads. She smiled, and he was hooked. He blurted out, "God, you're beautiful."

Maggie reached for the rose. Their fingers touched. She noticed how cute he looked.

"Liar," she said, smiling and blushing.

She was not used to compliments, especially from cute young men. Maggie stood up. "You're bleeding. A thorn must have pricked your finger."

He didn't know what to say, so he licked the trickle of blood and she laughed out loud!

"I've seen you before. Do you live around here?" she asked.

He cleared his throat, "Around the corner," and pointed with his thumb over his shoulder to a narrower alleyway.

"Well, I gotta go," she said, and walked away.

He turned, watching her as she went, and saw her half turn and look back at him. They both smiled at one another, and she kept going.

"Hey," Dave caled out. "What's your name?"

"Maggie," she called, turning around. "What's yours?"

"Dave," he said, as she turned the corner with a smile on his face. At last he knew her name and had spoken to her.

Maggie had seen Dave a few times before with his mother. She thought he was cute. She and her sister had met his mother the previous September in the park. Mrs. Bell was feeding pigeons when the sisters smiled at her. She walked over to them and began talking.

"You two live on Lovett Way, don't you? Me and my boy live down a ways from you, I'm Mrs. Bell," she said.

Maggie and her sister introduced themselves and exchanged knowing glances—*so that was the good looking boy's last name—Bell.*

The winter snows had finally melted; the April rains had ceased. Everything looked clean, and most of the soot had washed away. East Ohio Street on the North Side of

Pittsburgh was busy with pedestrian traffic, and Dave was on his way home to Lovett Way, one of the more narrow streets, which most people called an alley. He turned up the walkway to the little white frame house, where he lived with his Mom, and wished he were back in Rural Valley, where they had lived before moving into town. Rural Valley was a peaceful farm community, not so busy and crowded like this 'Burgh. He couldn't seem to breathe here, or find enough space or air, or even trees. The West Park had trees, but it just wasn't the same as living in the country. *Well, Dave thought, I could borrow a rowboat from the old guy down the street. I'll take the boat down to the Allegheny River for some fresh air. Surely the soot and grime of the city would not loom over the river. Why, I could even take my sister Millie with me.*

The next day, Dave got the rowboat from the man everyone called Old Granny. Since Millie's husband was away working in Washington, D.C., she was happy to accept Dave's invitation to go for a boat ride. But, she told him she would have to bring her three-year-old son, Frankie along.

Dave thought a boat ride would be fun for little Frankie and he had another passenger in mind for his river adventure—Maggie, the pretty girl down on Lovett Way. In spite of a bad case of nerves, Dave headed down the block and soon he was in front of Maggie's house, knocking at the door.

Maggie answered the front door and looked into a set of dazzling blue eyes.

"Hi, Dave."

At first Dave was tongue-tied. Her smile mesmerized him. His heart started to pound.

"Cat got your tongue?" she said.

Dave cleared his throat. "A-hem, a... Maggie," he sputtered out. "Maggie! My sister Millie and her son Frankie and I are going for a boat ride down the Allegheny this afternoon. Would you like to come with us?"

"I'm helping my mother with the housecleaning. As much as I'd like to go, I have to say no. Thanks anyway. Say, where'd you get the boat? I know you don't have one."

"Old Granny lent me his rowboat."

"Well, you be careful, David. That boat must as old as Old Granny."

As Maggie watched him go down the street, her heart fluttered. She knew Dave really liked her, and she felt the same about him. She liked his build, strong, well-muscled; but she wished he wasn't so young. Why he must be at least two or three years younger than she was, and she was almost twenty-one. Just the same, she liked the way his shaggy black hair fell over his forehead, and liked the cute way he kept pushing it back with his hand to keep it in place. He had the deepest blue eyes, and the handsomest face she ever saw. She sighed, and went back in the house. Dave would be easy to love, but... he was so young.

Chapter 2
River Tragedy

Millie was delighted that her brother Dave asked her to go for a ride with him on the river. He didn't mind at all that she was taking her little Frankie with them. She didn't often get to go anywhere but shopping, or visiting their mother, or their sister Mary. This would be a great adventure, going on a boat with Dave.

Millie was wide and short, but not fat. Her hair was thin and dark and she always wore it in a hairnet. She was a quiet person, who took good care of her little boy, helped her mother, and kept a clean house in spite of the Pittsburgh grime that seemed to be everywhere.

"Get into the boat Millie. Careful now." Dave held it steady as she got in, and lifted Frankie onto her lap.

"Do you know how to drive one of these things, Davey?"

"Don't worry, Mil, I won't let you drown."

Millie laughed at this. She was glad to be doing something different for a change. She was wishing her husband, Frank, could enjoy this with them. Well, it would be nice to go down the river, see the sights. There were so many boats on the river. Dave pushed the boat off, jumped in, and took the oars in his capable hands.

"Looks like the soot is on the river too, Mil.

There's no getting away from it."

Millie watched, mesmerized by the dip and rise motion of the oars, and the lap, lap, slap of the water against the sides of the little craft. She had never been in a rowboat before. It was nice, soothing. Everything looked different from down on the water. As they got toward the middle of the river, Millie noted the rowboat rocking a little more, and the water started slapping the boat a little harder.

"Davey, Davey, what's happening?" She felt an unexplained fear.

Frankie thrust his arms in the air. Pointing his finger, he exclaimed loudly, "Lookie, Mommy, lookie, big boat!"

"Davey, you see that big one over there?" She pointed to the white double-decker paddle-wheeler coming toward them. "Look." She saw the big riverboat; it was huge. The rowboat began to roll; Millie was frightened.

"Hey, Mil, hold on tight, hold on to Frankie, we're going to get rocked hard by that big one. It's coming close. Oh, shit!"

The little rowboat started to rock up and down like a seesaw as it crested the waves thrown by the big paddle-wheeler. Dave tried back rowing fast to get out of its way, but as the big riverboat came closer, and passed them, it threw a ton of water in its wake, and the hapless little rowboat rocked wildly. Dave yelled and lunged forward to grab his sister and nephew as his boat started rolling over with the force of the waves. It was a nightmare. Water covered his head and his ears clogged as he went under. All he could think of was Millie and Frankie.

Millie couldn't swim. He had offered to teach her many

times when they lived on the farm. But she always refused saying she was too busy. Dave spit and sputtered the foul tasting water from his mouth. He took a deep breath and dove under to grab Millie. She was holding Frankie. Dave grabbed her arm but his hold on her slipped.

"Oh God, oh God!"

He shot upward, took another deep breath, and spotted her again. She bobbed up, and grabbed one of Dave's legs, With one arm, she held Frankie close to her chest. Dave yelled to her to hold tight, and swam forward as best he could with her weight pulling on him. With burning lungs and aching arms he struggled toward a stationary barge near the shore.

When at last, he reached the stationary barge, it was filled with coal and was sunk low in the filthy water. This made it possible for Dave to swing his arm up over the barge and hang on for dear life while keeping his legs wrapped around Millie as she clung to the baby.

It felt like the rough edge of the barge was cutting into his arm. He was freezing, and his arm felt numb. He hoped someone would come to help them.

Millie was terrified for her baby.

"Hold tight to him" she told herself. "Hold on! I have to hold on."

She tried to tell herself she would be okay. She could feel Davey's legs wrapped around her middle. She heard a whistle blow—long and loud like a foghorn. It blew again and again. She could hear a train somewhere in the distance. She began to shiver. She smelled the putrid water, the smoke from the hams and bacon of Herr's Island

sickened her. She thought of the pigs and cattle slaughtered when they slid down Pig's Run to the island. The thought made her feel faint. She looked down at her baby. Frankie had stopped struggling. His cries had stopped. He was burbling. "Why doesn't Davey get us out of the water?" Frankie felt so heavy. "What was Davey saying." she thought. He seemed to be shouting. "What was he shouting?"

"Davey," Millie cried, " I can't hold on to the baby much longer," she said in a weak voice.

She felt Davey tighten his grip on her. She couldn't hold on to Frankie. Why? He felt so heavy. Suddenly he fell out of her grasp. She watched him go into the water. Then everything went black. Millie had fainted.

"Oh God," Dave shouted again and again. "Someone help! Help us!"

Dave watched in helpless horror as Little Frankie disappeared in the murky water. Dave was holding on tight to the barge. His arm felt raw. Millie suddenly felt heavier—like dead weight. "She must have passed out," he thought. Dave willed himself not to let go.

The water was green and putrid. "Damn boat! Why didn't someone come," thought Dave. "Anyone! God help us, *please!*" he prayed. Again and again he called out, "HELP! HELP!"

At last, someone on shore spotted them and ran to get the policeman who patrolled the area. The police came in a van. A few people gathered on the shore.

" There's someone hanging onto a barge out in the river, Sarge. I saw their boat flip over."

"Go on down and tell them help is on the way."

There was a lot of confusion along the river not far from the Heinz plant. There were fire trucks, police vans, ambulances, sirens screaming, people chattering.

"What happened?"

"A rowboat overturned. I think somebody drowned."

"That old guy over there called an ambulance."

"Here it comes now."

Meanwhile, in the river, Dave's arm was locked onto the coal barge. He was still holding on to the unconscious Millie with his legs, scissor fashion. Dave did not even hear the sirens. Someone untangled his arms and legs and pulled him out of the water. Someone pulled Millie out. Both were lifted onto the shore.

People watched as they lifted the woman out of the water, then the man. A fireman started to revive Millie. She came to, and screamed "My baby, Frankie, my boy, Frankie!"

Someone sat Dave onto an old crate and threw a blanket around his shoulders. A woman in a Salvation Army uniform took his hands and wrapped them around a cup of steaming coffee. Lifting his boyish face, he looked up at his rescuer and said, matter-of-factly, "The baby fell into the water."

"Baby? What baby? We didn't see any baby."

Dave rose from the crate and threw off his blanket.

"Cripes, the baby... her baby!" He points to Millie. "Didn't you see the baby?"

He was angrily pushing everyone out of the way as he tried to get back to the river but the policemen stopped him and pulled him back.

"We'll send in a diver. Calm down, buddy. We'll find the kid."

Upon hearing there was a child in the water, a stranger dove in, intent upon finding the boy. He came up after a minute, not seeing anything. He shouted to a policeman who was on shore, "Nothing there. I didn't see the child."

He dove in several times, coming up for air. Finally, he pulled himself out of the water and walked a few short steps to an officer, dripping wet.

Dark clouds gather and it began to drizzle.

Revived, but in shock, Millie is lifted onto a stretcher and put into the ambulance. A policeman took Dave by the arm and ushered him inside with his sister.

"Come on fella, up you go."

The ambulance took off for Allegheny General Hospital with sirens screaming.

Opening the newspaper the next day, there is an article on the front page of the *Sun Telegraph*. It tells of the drowning of the little boy, and the rescue of his mother by her brother and their rescue by the police and firemen.

The accident was covered on the news that night on KDKA radio.

"My goodness, Maggie," Pauline exclaimed when she heard the news about what happened.

They were gathered in Maggie's family kitchen the day following the accident.

"Aren't you glad you didn't go with Dave? How

terrible. I'm so afraid of the water. I'd never go near the river! Never!"

In those days the Rossi household didn't have a telephone, so Maggie had to pay a call in person to express her sorrow at the terrible thing that happened.

"Pauline, I'm going to Dave's to see if there is anything we can do for them. You want to come?"

"Yes. Wait 'till I tell Mama where we're going."

"Gosh, Maggie, I just can't believe that little boy drowned. Oh, gosh. Poor Millie."

"Poor Dave. I can't imagine how terrible he feels. Thank God he got Millie out safe."

Maggie and Pauline arrived at Dave's home, and knocked on the door. They could hear someone inside. They knocked again, several times.

Mrs. Bell finally opened the door. She squinted in the bright sun of the day.

"Who's there?"

"It's us, Mrs. Bell. Is Dave home?"

"Come in, come in. No, he's down at the river. They've sent men, divers, to look for Frankie."

Her face immediately crumpled and her shoulders shook as tears streamed down her face. She turned away from them for a moment as she wiped her tears then said, "Come sit at the table. I have coffee made. You drink coffee?"

Maggie and Pauline looked at each other. They really didn't want any, but they thought if they sat at the table with Mrs. Bell, it would help steady her, so they sat down. Asking about Millie, they were told she was released from

the hospital. Mrs. Bell said that Frank had been notified by the Red Cross as to what had happened. He was flying in tonight from Washington, D.C.

Someone opened the door. Dave shuffled in.

"Dave"

Maggie couldn't say anything else. She didn't need to, because of the look on his face.

"They haven't found his body."

After having coffee and offering any help the family might need, Maggie and Pauline went home.

Maggie heard a knock on the kitchen door. She opened it to see Dave standing there, alone.

He needed to see her, touch her, to receive some consolation and comfort. He is encouraged as she takes his hand and pulls him into the warm, inviting kitchen.

"They found him, under the barge."

"Oh, David, I'm so sorry."

They sit and talk about the accident—the terrible loss.

Maggie asks, "When will he be laid out?"

"I'm not sure. We have to go make arrangements yet. Probably tomorrow, since it's too late tonight."

He hangs his head and turns away from Maggie. He wants so much to take her in his arms, to lay his head on her shoulder, nuzzle her neck. But he doesn't; he is not quite sure of her feelings for him, doesn't know how she will respond. After all, he hasn't known her all that long, although it seems to him he as known her forever, at least in his dreams.

"I feel so bad for Millie and Frank. And you... oh, Dave."

Maggie did have feelings for Dave, but wasn't quite sure what to say, so she said nothing and just held his hand to comfort him.

Dave nodded his head as if to agree.   Words are stuck in his throat.

"Dave, when do you have to leave for CCC camp?"

"I almost forgot about that. Soon, I think. They told me I have to go by train to Ft. Meade in Maryland first; then they'll assign me to a camp. I just hope it's near Pittsburgh, so I can get home to see you, Maggie. I'll miss you."

He put his arm around her waist and turned toward her. He reached up, touched her hair, kissed her soft cheek, her temple, and leaned his head into her hair to drink in the fresh fragrance of it. He pulled her closer but she pushed him away slightly.

They both knew that this isn't the time.   The death of little Frankie had clouded everything.

She was embarrassed, but some part of her knows that she liked the feel of him, the smell of him, the idea of love. *Oh my*, she thinks, *love? Is this love?*

"Dave –"

She kissed him back. Reluctantly, before things went any further, she said, "You'd better go now."

He kissed her one more time and left.

The newspaper headline in the *Sun Telegraph*:

TRAGEDY STRIKES — THREE-YEAR-OLD DROWNS IN ALLEGHENY RIVER

Three-year-old Frank Madden Jr. drowned Saturday afternoon while on a boat ride with his mother, Millie Madden, and his uncle, David Bell. A riverboat going up river caused waves that overturned the small craft. David, a strong young eighteen-year-old swimmer, held on to his sister while she held on to her son. Millie passed out, and Little Frankie fell into the cold, dark waters of the Allegheny.

Our brave Pittsburgh Police and Firemen came to their rescue as passersby looked on. All three victims were taken to Allegheny General Hospital. All victims were residents of the North Side. The Salvation Army was also at the scene to hand out hot coffee to all."

Little Frankie's Funeral

No one can imagine the death of their little one. It isn't right that a child dies before its parents. At the same time, it isn't fair that a parent dies while the child is still young. No one prepares for these tragedies, no one.

Millie and Frank made arrangements at the nearby Sirlin Funeral Home. Dave, their mother, and their other sister, Mary, went along for support. They all walked solemnly toward the East Ohio Street funeral home. The parish priest from St. Mary's met them there. He was a kindly priest. He was the one who informed them that the divers had found the body.

Frank Senior was devastated by the death of his son. Little Frankie was all he lived for. Every day he looked forward to coming home from a hard day's work to see his happy and smiling son. Now his son was gone. Dead. Horrible word. He could not blame Millie. He could not blame Dave. He only felt a deep sadness and emptiness. *Now what?* There were no words to express how he felt. He arose in the morning, got dressed, and shaved. Even a morning shower did not refresh him. He felt like a sleepwalker.

The morning of the funeral, he thought he could not go through with it. Perhaps if he pretended it was not his child lying in the small casket, he could get through it. He would try.

Outside the window birds were chirping. He could hear people moving around in the apartment downstairs; someone's radio was on. The very air seemed to have life, but Frank did not.

Millie came into the bedroom. She went into his arms and just held him, trying to find some comfort. She looked up at him.

"How are we supposed to do this? I can't stand it. Tell me it really didn't happen, Frank. It's all a nightmare, isn't it… a bad dream?"

She pushed away from his embrace throwing herself on the bed in despair. Millie sank her face into her hands, shaking her head from side to side, her body convulsing with sobs.

Frank looked at her helplessly. He did not know what to do. He was in the same state himself.

"Mil," he said, as sat down beside his wife and took her hand, putting his other arm around her back. "We have to go, we'll get through it. Mil, we will."

Hundreds of people flooded the funeral home to offer consolation to the parents and to each other. They had tears in their eyes as they viewed the tiny casket holding Little Frankie Madden. Friends, relatives, and many concerned strangers attended to give consolation and offer sympathy.

Frank Madden entered the funeral home's front door. He began to feel lightheaded. He couldn't seem to take it all in. Why were there so many people here? When he had left the house last week to go to work, his little boy was sleeping soundly. He could still see his child, his little boy, the light of his life, and he was looking forward to playing with him and taking him to the park to play when he got back home.

Approaching the room in which the casket lay, he saw the roster with the name Frank Madden Jr. He stopped. He looked up. He could feel everyone's eyes on him. He stepped into the room. He stepped up to the closed casket, looked at the photograph of his son above the casket and collapsed.

Throughout the funeral, and the burial, friends and relatives filled the house,while Millie and Frank just sat through the nightmare of days.

Frankie Madden was buried up on the hill in the family plot.

Millie wished for the past, before Frankie had become a memory. She and Frank Senior went to the cemetery every day; sometimes Frank couldn't get Millie to leave.

Millie could not accept that little Frankie, whom she had birthed, fed, changed, held and loved was gone. Oh, what she wouldn't give to have her son back.

Frank would live only two years more. He died of a heart attack, but some people said it was from a broken heart. He was laid to rest beside his beloved son. Millie coped as best as she could, but she was lonely and lost without her son and husband. Finally she went to live with her sister Mary, up the hill on Brushton Avenue.

Chapter 3
The Lovers

The lovers sat on the front steps of Maggie's house. It was twilight, a night made for romance. The summer moon could be seen peeking above the housetops in the narrow street; it was high above in the darkening sky, and the stars twinkled overhead. There was a slight breeze.

Although there was a little cooling breeze, Dave thought it was generally stifling in the city. He wished for the fresh country air of Rural Valley, where he was born and lived for the first years of his life.

When Maggie and I marry, he thought, *we'll move out into the country somewhere.*

"How soon will you be leaving for camp?" Maggie asked, leaning toward David.

"Pretty soon, Maggie. I don't know exactly."

"We won't have much more time to be together, David. I'm going to miss you so much!"

He touched her face gently. "Maggie. I love you." He reached out to take her hand, and pulled her up from the steps. Hand in hand, walking closely and silently, they headed toward the park. Bright stars blinked overhead and the night sounds of the city filled the air. They walked slowly, their hearts fluttering like the leaves of the Sycamore trees that lined the path. As they near a park bench, Dave stopped. Maggie turned, and looked at him questioningly. She had this feeling that he was going to ask her to marry him. And she was not quite ready for this.

"Maggie," he whispered, and tenderly looked down at her upturned face. He drew back. He let go of her hand and reached into his jacket. He removed a pack of Camels from his shirt pocket. With exasperating slowness, he tapped the pack on his knuckles and took out a cigarette, and put it between his lips. Then, striking the match along the abrasive dark stripe, he cupped his hands around the small fire, and finally touched the flame to the tip. As he inhaled a deep, satisfying puff of the cigarette, his eyes met Maggie's; he smiled.

Putting her hands on her hips, her feelings changed; she suddenly felt frustrated and angry.

"A cigarette!" she exclaimed. A cigarette!"

She was expecting a ring, a declaration of love, a proposal of marriage-something other than a cigarette! She nearly exploded with anger and disappointment.

But then he took another puff, reached into his jacket pocket, and withdrew a small box and handed it to her. She smiled then, and calmed down. This was more like it. Opening up the box, she saw a small diamond set in a gold band. She did not know what to say. It was beautiful.

He could not find the right words to express what he wanted to say. He cleared his throat. "A-hem! A-a-a—well, it's a ring," he said.

Dave was a man of few words; that is, when faced with strong emotions, he sometimes had difficulty expressing himself.

"Silly," I know that."

She had calmed down considerably. Maggie looked up at him expectantly.

His eyes fixed on her rosy cheeks, blue eyes, and wavy brown hair. He knew what he wanted to say, but it was easier thinking it than putting it into words. Taking action, he put his hands firmly on her shoulders, pulling her toward him, and kissed her on the forehead. Maggie's skin felt so soft and warm. He moved his lips downward and kissed the tip of her nose. He sought her lips and lingered there, tasting her sweetness.

At first, she closed her eyes at the sudden rush of feeling that welled up inside her, then realizing they were in a public park, opened her eyes wide and pulled away.

"David –"

She looked up, waiting for him to say I love you, but the moment passed, and she just waited for him to say something.

Staring at her, the words stuck in his chest.

Finally he blurted out, "Maggie, will you marry me?"

Suddenly he felt relieved; the question was out at last.

But Maggie ignored what her heart told her—that she loved him—and her head took over.

Fighting her feelings, and hoping he would understand, she finally said, "Dave, you don't even know me well enough to ask me to marry you. You don't know me at all. And, I don't really know enough about you to make such a serious commitment. When you come back home on leave, we'll talk about it then. We both need time, Dave, time to get to know each other."

She felt agitated. Her feelings were mixed, pulling her both ways. She loved him, didn't she? Did it matter that he was younger? She wasn't sure. After all, he was only two years younger. Maybe she could talk to her sister Pauline about it.

Although Dave didn't say the words 'I love you,' she knew and felt in her heart, that he did.

She couldn't keep still. Excitement was coursing through her body. She felt the need to move. She put her arm through Dave's, pulling him along, and started walking out of the park, toward the lighted shops along the avenue.

"Let's walk. I need to think."

Dave was disappointed. His shoulders drooped.

"Hold on a minute," he said, wresting his arm from hers.

He took the cigarette from his mouth and dropped it on the ground. Looking at it, he crushed it out thoroughly with the toe of his shoe. He did not know what to say. He was sure Maggie loved him. He felt it in the way she spoke to him, the way she returned his kisses, the way she looked at him. Now what? It was painful to take rejection, especially since he was fairly sure she returned his feelings of love. What could he say? What could he do? He realized she was walking away, and called to her.

"Maggie! Maggie, stop. Please, wait."

She stopped, waited, and turned around slowly toward him.

He closed up the short distance between them. In desperation, he put his hands on her arms. The words came pouring out of him.

"Maggie, I know you love me. I love you, I always will. What's the matter? Is it because I can't be here with you,

because I'm going away? When I come home from camp I'll get a job. Is it because I don't have a job? Is that why?"

He took out another cigarette and lit it. The thought struck him that she didn't say no. So there was hope that some day she might say yes. They started walking.

"Dave, you know I like you a lot. I feel great being with you. You make me happy to be with you. But there are other things to consider, not the least of which you are younger than I, and you don't have a job. Besides, my family counts on the money I bring home too. There's that to consider. Dave, I will think about it. But we do have to discuss this.

As she walked along with him, Maggie wondered where he got the money for the ring. Dave, however, was glad that she didn't ask that question because he didn't want to admit to her that he had earned it by collecting bets for a bookie.

"I'm sure I'll get a job when I get back. Say, do you like the ring, even though it's not a big diamond?"

As she tried the ring on her finger, the feelings she had for him welled up inside her and she stretched up on tiptoe and kissed him quickly on the cheek.

"I love you, Dave. The ring—the size of the diamond is fine, but I still have to think about marriage. It's such a big step. I really hadn't considered that at all, especially now, when the whole country is in difficulty. We're lucky we have enough to eat; you know how things are these days."

"You don't have to tell me. I've seen the bread lines."

He glanced down at the ring on her finger, lifted up the hand on which she had just placed it, and held it up. Jokingly, he said, "I could return it and get you one from a gumball machine, or out of a Cracker Jack box."

She saw his glance and immediately relaxed and smiled. "I'll just keep this one until I make up my mind."

"While you're thinking, sweetheart, remember what I said."

"What, Dave, what did you say?"

She knew he meant that he loved her, but she wanted him to say it.

"You know."

He just couldn't get the words out, but he knew that she knew.

"We'd better be getting back home. It is getting late."

And she wanted to show her mama the ring.

Chapter 4

Going to Camp

June 26, 1934
Hello, sweet, I finally got to Camp Meade, Maryland,
after starting from Union Station at 11:41 A.M. Thursday.
There are several thousand tents here.

*D*ave was on the train, on the way to Ft. Meade, Maryland, along with several other recruits. He finally arrived at his destination, and we next see him waiting for his physical exam and inoculation shots.

At the Induction Center at Fort Meade, Maryland, all the men were sitting on benches or chairs in a wide hallway, waiting for the exam by the doctor.

An aide yelled, and drawled out loudly, "Ne-e-e-xt!"

He is holding a check chart.

Dave slowly rose from his bench. He was shirtless. He walked up to the aide who called out.

"Come on, fella, we don't have all day. What's your name?"

"David Bell," he said, spelling out his last name.

"Age and birth date?"

"Eighteen. January 9, 1916."

"A'rite. Go through that door," the aide said, pointing with a pencil. "Ne-e-e-xt!"

Dave went through the door to the examining room. The

doctor checked his blood pressure, heart, looked in his mouth, eyes, ears.

"Stand up. Drop your pants."

Dave stopped. His eyebrows shot up and he looked at the doctor in disbelief.

"Do you want me to do it for you?" the doctor says sarcastically.

Dave unbuttoned and unzipped his trousers and let them fall down.

"Turn around."

Dave turned.

"Okay, now bend over and touch your toes."

Glaring, he bent down.

"Pull 'em up," the doctor says, after visually checking Dave for spinal alignment.

Greatly relieved, Dave pulled up his trousers and turned around.

The doc handed Dave a slip. "Give this to the quartermaster," he said, and points his thumb over his shoulder to the opposite door.

Dave went down a long hallway to another room to get his gear (new clothing, army issue, of course, but left over from WWI, as he later finds out), about thirty pounds worth, and is told to return to his tent to change. Dave came out of the quartermaster's door carrying an armload of khaki pants and shirts, with a pair of shoes on top. He walked out and over to his assigned tent. Each of the tents held thirty cots and on that hot afternoon the temperature inside read one-hundred seventeen degrees.

Dave plopped down his army issue clothes and looked

around to see who was there. After putting his clothes away in his footlocker, he decided to finish writing his letter to Maggie, as he has an hour before dinner. As he wrote, a bead of sweat rolled down his nose and dropped onto the paper. He swiped at it with the back of his hand and decided it would be best to shower before finishing his letter.

Refreshed after a shower and change of clothes,but hungry, Dave reclined on his cot to finish writing to Maggie.

June 26, 1934

We received about 30 lbs. of clothes today and I had to carry them in one hundred seventeen-degree heat. We also had our physical exam today, and my arm sure is sore. We received two injections today and have to have two more. I expect to leave for regular camp, and I don't know where, but I don't think it will be near Pittsburgh.

Love, Dave

At the camp at Ft. Meade, the men are hardened by exercising, and are required to attend lectures on what is expected of them and what the CCC is all about. They learned it is about the conservation and preservation of forestlands. After only a few weeks of training and lectures, they are rerouted to their final destinations.

Dave writes again to Maggie.

July 30, 1934

Dear Maggie,

I found out we are to leave Tuesday, but I don't know where. You can't get definite information from anyone, because the officers in charge won't tell you.

Dave

Central Pennsylvania Counties

Dave is being sent to Camp Malone, "Tea Springs." All mail sent to him is addressed to Loganton, Pennsylvania.

Loganton is in Central Pennsylvania, at the southern end of Clinton County, near Centre County. Camp Malone, Tea Springs Company 368, Camp #S114, is in Union County where the counties of Clinton, Centre, and Union meet—looking like pie wedges on the map.

August 1934

Dave and a dozen other enrollees, all dressed in the official khaki uniform of the CCC, were on the train, speeding off to the Pennsylvania National Forest. When they got off, they found themselves in a town named Jersey Shore, Pennsylvania. But there is no shore, just mountains and rocks and trees. Soon they are loaded onto a truck that took them past Lock Haven and Rauchtown to Loganton. Loganton is located in the Sugar Valley area of Clinton County, in the Bald Eagle Mountains, named for Chief Logan's brother, Bald Eagle.

Dave felt lucky to be sitting near the open back of the truck because he is able to stare in wonderment at the wide meadows, high mountains, and dense forests. When they passed a deep meadow in the middle of the high hills, the truck driver explained that this area is called Sugar Valley. Dave would always remember how the cool, mountain air smelled earthy and sweet—scented with blue, yellow, and white wild flowers.

After many miles of travel, the truck turned onto a dirt road that took them through even denser forests towering overhead. It seemed to Dave as though the truck was passing through dark tunnels of one hundred-foot-high trees, shutting out all light, closing in on them like the darkest night, then suddenly opening up to a view of bluish-white light on far-off mountains reaching to the sky. It was like standing on the edge of a huge bowl and looking down into a lake, though there was no lake, only a beautiful meadow stretching far and wide.

At last they came to a level area and stopped. Everyone scrambled out to get a first look at the camp where they will spend the next several months.

Dave noticed the large camp sign, which reads, Camp Malone, Tea Springs. As he looked around, he saw several wooden buildings. The largest was marked Recreation Hall and Mess. There was an outdoor fireplace,the officers' quarters, and administration offices.

There were three galvanized trash cans near the fireplace, which stood on a large square of cement. Dave is told that two of the cans are used by the men for washing and rinsing their own metal dishes and utensils, and the other is used for trash.

After they were shown around camp and allowed to deposit their gear in the barracks, the men were ushered to the mess hall, where they ate a full meal. Everyone was amazed at the great quantities of good delicious food. Most of them did not get three square meals a day back home. Dave and the other men were also impressed with the cleanliness and orderliness of the camp.

Soon after they had settled in, Dave took the first opportunity he got, to write to Maggie. Laying on his bunk, he was interrupted by the fellow next to him.

"Who are you writing to, buddy? We've only been here two days and that's the third letter you've written!"

"My girl," he answered without looking up.

"Ooooh, must be nice. What's she like? I bet she's a real doll, do you have a picture?"

"No. I mean, she is nice, and no, I don't have a picture." Thinking the guy had better shut up and let him finish the letter.

August 1, 1934

Dear Maggie:

I finally arrived at Tea Springs, Union County, Tuesday at 3 o'clock P.M., after getting up at 3 A.M. in Maryland, and starting at 7:15 A.M. I am in the Pennsylvania State Park, and it sure is a mountain country. It's so cold in the night that we have three and four army blankets and still are cold. It's cold up till about 9 A.M. I start to work from one in the afternoon till eight at night. There are also other shifts from

4 A.M. till 12, and 8 till 4. I think they change each week. We were building a stone wall for an explosive shed today, and cutting trees. I am about 198 miles from Pittsburgh and about 14 miles from the railroad. The nearest store is about 4 miles away. It's hot in the day, but it's about 48 degrees at night. It's a great place, nothing but mountains and forests, and plenty of snakes, which you like.

Dave

Chapter 5

Back to Pittsburgh on a Two-Day Pass

*D*ave and Maggie embraced. They were so glad to see each other after a three-month separation. Maggie has realized how much she missed Dave. She has a million questions, and as usual, he just wants to spend time with her, not answer questions, but he does, in between trying to soften her up with hugs and kisses.

"I love what you write in your letters, David, about the mountain sunsets, the beauty of the forest, the poor little squirrels that you unmercifully catch and torture."

"Say, I told you I did not torture that squirrel. I rescued it from the cat that caught it. When I put it in my jacket, it bit me. It still hurts, look."

Dave showed Maggie his thumb, where the squirrel bit it.

She kissed his thumb. "Does it feel better now, dear?" She relented and softened up.

After too short a leave, Dave is off to Camp again.

Chapter 6

September Rainstorm at Camp

The men were on a detail up the mountain in Bald Eagle Forest when it started to rain. They were removing Quinceberry bushes in order to prevent blister rust from destroying the pine trees.

"Come on, fellas, we're going back to camp."

"Hey, Sarge, it's raining!"

"Gee, no kidding, buddy! Who told you?" he said sarcastically.

"Come on, fellas, we're going back to camp. It's raining too steady to do any work today. At least we got in half a day. I don't think it's going to stop anytime soon."

Luckily, they had been trucked up the mountain today, so they had a ride down.

Back in camp, Dave begins a letter to Maggie.

"Dear Maggie,

It's raining cats and dogs here. It rained all day Friday, but we worked a half day today, until it started raining again.

He had to stop writing when Fergie called out to him.

"Hey, Dave, ya gotta look at this, Dave."

Fergie stood in the open doorway.

"Outside, I mean … look! The stream looks like it's rising."

Dave stops writing, goes to the barracks door, lights a cigarette, looks out.

"Yer darn tootin', Ferg. It's going to be a mess."

Their mutual buddy, Frank McQuade, splashed through the rain up to the open door where they are standing. He began to speak as if he didn't even notice the rain or the puddle he was standing in.

"You guys going to join me for a great meal this evening?"

"Yeah, yeah," said Fergie.

"Wear your best tuxedos, and I shall call for a limousine," said McQuade with a hoity-toity accent.

"Hear, hear," answered Dave. "I think we may have to wear swim trunks."

They mess call sounded and they walked to the recreation hall for their supper.

"Hey, Dave, when are you going to show me a picture of your girl?" shouted the guy sitting down the table from Dave. He is stuffing meatballs into his mouth. His cheeks are so full, he looks like a chipmunk.

Dave looked down the table at this guy, and took an instant dislike to him.

"Just watch me," Dave told his buddies.

Dave wondered how he should handle this: *should I say never; or I don't have one; or if I did, I wouldn't show it to you; or when the cows come home*. He'd really like to say, "WHEN YOU STOP STUFFING YOUR FACE," but the guy would most likely misconstrue his meaning, and think he meant when he stopped eating his supper.

But before he got a chance to say anything, the guy yelled,, "Come on, Dave, is she that bad lookin', you have to hide her picture?"

Dave jumped up so fast he knocked his chair over. He had a quick temper.

"Aw, come on Dave," said his friend, McQuade. "He's an idiot. Don't let him get your goat. He don't even have a girl."

After a minute of glaring at him, Dave sat down and wiped his mouth. The guy who said that about his girl was smart enough to shut up.

When supper was over, the three buddies left the mess hall with their plates and mugs. Even though it was raining, they scraped their dishes into the trash and washed them in a hurry in the galvanized can provided for this. They rinsed them off in the next can. Each man had his own mess kit and had to clean it himself. As he was rinsing his cup, Dave noticed the water rising from the stream. McQuade voiced Dave's thoughts.

McQuade said, "Looks like the stream might overflow if it doesn't stop raining. Say, do you have any magazines I could look at Dave? I don't have nothin' else to do tonight."

"Yeah, Maggie sent me two new ones."

Dave entered his barracks and handed a magazine to McQuade. Then he stretched out on his bunk, comfortably full after his meal. His thoughts turn to Maggie; he missed her so much, especially now, when he is in bed, so comfortable and lazy. He decided to leave the unfinished letter to her for tomorrow, as he didn't feel like writing. Even though it's early evening, he dosed off, with visions of

a smiling brown-haired girl in his dreams.

Upon awakening the next morning, he found the rain has come down all night, and the water was up to the door.

Sept. 19, 1934

Dear Maggie,

To continue my letter that I started last week —

It rained all day Sat. night and all day Sunday until Sun. night, and it just poured down. All the streams overflowed and the one near the shower house and recreation hall came up to the steps. The company street looked like a pond. Plenty of dirt had to be shoveled away on Monday. Some of the mountain roads were washed out, and there sure is plenty work.

It's been pretty cold since, and we've had to wear lumber jackets, which we just got with some other winter supplies, including a comforter, which is an inch thick, and another army blanket and overcoat.

I had just received my raincoat the day before it rained and I sure did make use of it.

We had a lecture on Monday by a man from Washington, D.C., who is listed in a book called "Who's Who?" He sure was good.

Well, you asked me if I'd done something wrong to get K.P. Well, no. We all get our turn at K.P. but if you do, do something wrong, you get put on K.P., which isn't so good.

I'm getting table waiter tomorrow, and everyone gets their turn at that too, and also guard.

Well, everyone's time is up at the end of this month and

we have to sign up again.

Quite a few signed up to quit at the end of the month and a new bunch is coming in soon.

The crew I'm on now is always building bridges, and we just finished one today.

Coming back to camp the other evening we saw a groundhog, and after passing it the foreman decided to catch it, but it got away. It sure was a big one.

There's plenty nuts up here and also squirrels, now don't misunderstand me. I don't mean the fellows.

Well, the fellows didn't get to go to Jersey Shore Sat., as the Capt. wouldn't take us, only the ballplayers.

Well, I'll let you know if I go to the Catholic Church Sunday. I think I will, since you asked me to.

Don't forget, you haven't written me a mile long letter yet.

My regards to the family and also your girlfriends.

Love, Dave

Meanwhile, back at work, early Monday morning, the camp looked a mess, with ankle deep water everywhere, having come up from the overflowing streams. They are called to formation, and received orders. Luckily, Dave didn't have to muck out the latrines, which is not a pleasant job. It stinks, to put it mildly. But he took pleasure in knowing the kid that made him mad at supper Saturday night got *that* job! Still, shoveling out all the muck that accumulated over the past three days of rain was no fun, just a hard job that had to be dealt with.

Then there were the mountain roads to be dealt with. But that was the commander's job. Dave did not have to worry until he was called to help.

Dave wondered what Maggie was doing today. He gave thought about her going to night school, and that guy, the chemistry teacher, she had mentioned in her last letter. She did write, if he was not mistaken, that the guy wanted to date her. *Wonder what he's up to? Probably no good.* He voiced his thoughts to Fergie, something he is not used to doing. But he was worried about someone stealing his girl. It wasn't that Maggie couldn't be trusted; but he didn't trust the other guy, especially because he didn't know him.

Chapter 7
The Chemistry Teacher

Although she was supposed to be paying attention at night school, Maggie couldn't help thinking about Dave. He just turned eighteen; she was nearly twenty-one. As much as she was attracted to him, she was cautious. She didn't know him that well. Yet the strong physical attraction and physical pull was there. Should she? Shouldn't she? She was going to have to confide in one of her sisters, probably Pauline. They were close in age, only two years' difference. And then there were her parents to consider, especially her papa. Was Dave the same religion as she, Catholic? What was his background? He certainly wasn't Italian—Bell was not an Italian name. She would have to ask him about his parents; she knew his Mother and sister. This was a predicament for her, as she knew how her parents felt about anyone in the family marrying someone not of their faith or nationality. She had very strong feelings about marrying someone of the same faith, but why must he be Italian? After all, this was America! She would talk to him. What faith was he? If he wasn't Catholic, she would have to convince him to switch. If they were ever going to marry in her church, he would have to be Catholic, wouldn't he? Oh. She raised both hands to her cheeks as she realized what she was thinking—marriage! And she hardly knew him. Oh my! She could feel the heat rising up to her face. She lowered her head, and hoped no one could see her. She just knew her face had turned pink thinking about Dave and marriage. The thoughts intruded uninvited.

She looked up from her desk. The chemistry teacher had stopped talking and was looking at her. His hand, with the chalk in his fingers, was poised in midair, as in a dream. All of a sudden, her ears registered the click of the chalk on the board as he started putting a symbol on it. Thankfully, he asked someone else to answer, gave the assignment, and then dismissed the class.

As she was gathering her wits, along with her books, he called out to her.

"Miss Rossi, don't leave yet. I want to talk to you."

Maggie walked up to the front of the classroom.

"Yes, Mr. Gordon?"

"Miss Rossi, did you hear the assignment? You seemed distracted. You may not have heard me."

"Yes, yes, of course. You want us to memorize all the symbols and what they stand for."

"No, Miss Rossi, not all the symbols, just the group of non-metals. And read the next chapter, the one on chemical reactions."

Maggie turned and hurried out of the classroom, her face aflame.

Christina waited for her best friend.

"Maggie, what did he want? He is *soooo* good looking. Gee, I'd just die if he called my name. My knees would turn to rubber. I don't think I could walk—I'd be so embarrassed. You looked so composed. What were you thinking? I'll bet your knees were knocking. God. Did he ask you out? 'Miss Rossi, I've fallen in love with you!'" Christina exaggerated. "'I want to take you in my arms and make out with you!' Oooh—Maggie, what did he want?"

"Christina ... kid," Maggie laughed. "You have such an imagination! He only wanted to know if I heard the homework assignment. He is good to look at, isn't he? It would be easy to fall for him. But, Teenie, you know how much I like Dave."

"Yes, but he's so far away. Would you go out with Mr. Gordon if he asked you?"

Maggie smiled at the thought of Mr. Gordon asking her out. If he did—Maggie's thoughts wandered, *Would she, or wouldn't she?* He wasn't married. He had graduated teachers' college only two years ago, the gossips said. And there was a gin party coming up soon—not that she drank gin, or anything like that—but? Hmm. Something to think about. Boy, that Christina had such a wild imagination.

The following day was Saturday, and Maggie was in her mother's kitchen, learning to bake bread, and having romantic thoughts of Dave.

"See, *primo*, first, you put the flour into the pan, like so!" said Mrs. Rossi.

She made a well in the flour, which was in a shallow enameled pan. The pan was white with a red border. She took a large cake of yeast out of the icebox and started to unwrap it.

"Migalena, fill up that small white pan with warm water …the one on the stove."

Maggie got the pan and filled it up from the tap. "Here, Mama."

Mama crumbled up the yeast into the warm water. She put salt into the flour pan, added the yeast water, and then said to Maggie, "You bless the bread. See, look. Like this." Mama then demonstrates how she blesses the bread. She blessed the bread with the sign of the cross, saying the words in Italian. Then she said, "Watch me," and flicks the flour into the yeast water, in a circular fashion, moving the large round pan around when she needed to. "See, then you mix with your hand, adding olive oil around the pan, outside of the flour, so it won't stick. Then you mix with your hand, like so, and punch it."

Maggie corrected her. "Knead it, Mama, knead it."

"*Si*, yes, yes, you knead it."

Mama smiled and laughed and started singing an old song, "The Butcher Boy," in Italian, as she kneaded the bread.

As Marggie watched her mother, her thoughts turned to David.

Mama looked at her, and stopped singing. As though Mama was reading her thoughts, she says, "How is David? You got a letter yesterday."

"He is like a gypsy, Mama, so far away from me. He wants to marry me, Mama."

"You love him, figlia mia?" (my daugher), asks Mama.

Mama turns to put the bread in the unlit oven to rise.

"I don't know," answered Maggie. "I'm not sure. You

know, Mama, he is a little younger than me. Besides, I don't know if I'm ready to marry anyone just yet."

Not that that has anything to do with her feelings of love for Dave.

Chapter 8
October 9, 1934

Hello David:

How's the world treating you? Did you get the 2 magazines I sent you? I hope the captain does not read them before he gives them to you, and I hope there is enough postage on them. Gosh, sweetheart, time sure does drag here with you gone. No matter where I go, I cannot enjoy myself. I suppose I think of you more than I should. Have you had any pictures of yourself taken yet? I mean without having your shoulders drooped. I am quite sure I told you that Anna, Christina, and myself are going to night school. It sure is cold in this old 'Burgh.

Gee, darling, I sure am glad that you didn't take that dynamiting job, for you say it is dangerous. I don't know what I would do if anything happened to you. Gosh, it is getting late and I am very sleepy. Regards from the family and friends. So long, sweet-heart, till the next letter.

Much Love, Maggie
P.S. Answer soon!

October 12, 1934
Loganton, PA

Hello, loveable,

I received your magazines and letter. I appreciate the magazines very much. It wasn't the captain who read the magazines before. It was the CCC First Sergeant, who has charge of the mail. Well, this week I've been working from 12:30 till 7:30 P.M., still on a new road. Part of the day, another fellow and I work together with our own gang, barring rocks.[3] The rest of the day we work with a tractor driver, hauling big rocks out of the road that can't be rolled out by the fellows. Here's one for you. As I said before, we were barring rock along the new road and the dynamiters were fixing a charge, which we didn't know about. So we see one dynamiter walk past us on a curve, out of sight, and we keep on working. We came within 25 feet of the charge, which we didn't know about. All at once, we hear the dynamiter at the other end yell for us to go back, as he was about to put off that charge. If it wasn't for him, we might have been hurt pretty bad by the charge. It was the dynamiter's fault who walked past us and didn't tell us to go back from the charge. He must have been daydreaming or something, but it wasn't so bad after all.

Say, you should see Mother Nature in all her splendor and beauty now. I never saw a forest more beautiful in my life. An artist could never paint a more beautiful piece of scenery. If you saw it, you would say the same.

By the way, the charge that was set off blasted out a lot of rattlesnakes, of which I am sending you one.

I hope you still love me as I do you.

Dave

What Dave didn't tell Maggie in the letter was that when he dove for cover, he got slightly injured. In fact, he got knocked out, as a rock flew onto his head, and he twisted his ankle when he jumped out of the way of the blast. The guy that was with him barring rock was also knocked out, and they ended up in the First Aid Station and Company Hospital. He didn't tell Maggie, because he did not want her to worry, or worse yet, get mad and ask him to come home. He liked the camp, the money, and best of all he enjoyed working in the forest.

Chapter 9

Maggie heard a knock at the door and answered it. The mailman handed her a box the size of a cigar box (eight by six by four). She took it into the kitchen and put it on the table and read the return address: D. Bell, Tea Springs Camp S114, Loganton, Pennsylvania. It had a stout cord around it. She had already gotten the letter in which Dave said he was sending her a rattlesnake, but of course, she didn't believe him. But now, as she looked at the box, she thought about it. Her sister walked into the room as Maggie shook the box and heard something moving inside.

"Who is it from, Dave? Did he send you a rattlesnake, like he promised? Ha ha ha!"

Maggie looked at her sister with a deadly glare in her eyes. "Would you like to open it and find out, DEAR SISTER? Since you read all my mail over my shoulder, maybe you would like to open the box?"

"It's your box, you open it! Dear Sister." She smiled and moved over to the doorway—just in case it was a live snake!

Maggie pulled the string of the bow slowly. She pulled off the string, holding the wrapping. She gently tore the brown paper, to reveal a cigar box. Then she cautiously lifted the lid—and screamed!!! Her sister screamed. Her mama and papa came running into the kitchen. Maggie, who had dropped the box onto the table, was speechless (unusual for her) and could only point to the box. When her Mama looked and immediately put her hands in a prayer-like fashion to heaven and said, "Madonna Mia!" Maggie's Papa reached into the box and pulled out the contents—a very long rattlesnake skin.

"It doesn't look like a cigar!" he said as he grinned—his face was red to the roots of his silver gray hair, his round belly shaking.

"Holy smokes!" said Maggie, "he really *did* send me a rattlesnake! Just wait till I get him, just wait!"

Chapter 10

*D*ave was hobbling around camp, on crutches,his ankle and foot wrapped up in a thick bandage. The bandage on his head was removed. He now had only a patch covering the spot where the rocks hit him on the forehead. Luckily, he did not have a concussion. When he fell back, he landed in a soft forest bed of pine needles.

"You going to the fair tonight in White Deer?"

"May as well, I can't do nothin' else with this foot like it is."

"Did you hear from your girl yet? Did she get the snakeskin you sent her?"

"I didn't hear from her yet; it's too soon."

Another buddy came to join them. They all climbed into the waiting truck and went to White Deer, to the fair. White Deer was a small community consisting of about ten houses and a church.

The men got out of the truck and walked to the field where the fair was set-up. They passed a tent with a sign outside that read, HAVE YOUR FORTUNE TOLD BY THE GYPSY.

"Hey, Dave, get your fortune told! Ask the Gypsy lady if that girl you write to all the time loves you."

"Yeah, especially when she gets that snakeskin."

"Yeah, Dave, it's only a nickel!"

58

"I don't believe in that stuff. You go in and get your fortune told. I'd rather try my luck with hitting the milk bottles."

"C'mon, Dave, I'll pay—you go in and see the Gypsy lady. Don't be chicken."

"I'm not chicken, I just don't want to."

They nudged him through the open flaps into the tent and followed in behind him. They all stood there just looking at the wizened old crone, who was sitting at a round table, with a crystal ball in front of her. She was wearing a shawl, and was very scary looking. She had gray strands of hair poking out of her dark red bandana, which was wrapped tightly around her head. Her thin nose was as crooked as her finger, long and pointed. Dave was fascinated by her eyes; they were so deeply penetrating, it seemed like they looked into his very soul. It was dark in her tent.

She waited for the young men to stop staring at her. "Vell. You have come to see Sylvia and have your fortune told? All of you? No, no, only one soldier at a time." She pointed a crooked finger at Dave. "Sit down. I tell your fortune."

Dave sat and the others left, standing outside her tent. "She is scary looking. Maybe we shouldn't have done it to him."

In the tent, Dave felt awkward. Even though there was no sound in the tent, the Gypsy crone said, "Be qviet, do not make a sound while I look into my crystal." She makes movements with her arms and hands over the glass ball. Dave looked bored. Then the lady says, "I see a girl." He began to pay attention.

"I see a girl with dark hair, short dark hair." Dave was still interested but was skeptical at this point because Maggie had long hair. The Gypsy continued. "She is standing in a hall, a school. A man is making looks at her. He is a smart looking man, wearing a suit, with books under his arms. The books have strange symbols on them. Oh, oh," she says, "the crystal is clouding over… I see smoke, and rock flying through the air, and trees falling. Someone is hurt." She looks at Dave. "Vas dat you?" she asks.

Dave looks at her. "Yeah, that was me. Me and my buddy. Tell me about this girl. What man was looking at her, tell me?"

"No more, I see no more. Vas that your girl I saw?"

Dave responds by getting up. "I don't know. My girl has long hair, not short hair." He grabbed his crutches and hopped out of the tent.

"Well, what did she say?"

"Nothing. She didn't say nothing."

"Aw, Dave, she did. Tell us. What did she say?"

"She said what she saw. She said I got hurt. She must have heard about the blasting. Any simpleton can see I'm hurt. Look at me. She saw the bandage on my foot. Let's go, I want to try my luck at hitting them rubber milk bottles!"

Dear Maggie,

The fellows and I went to a fair at White Deer on Saturday. There was a dance afterward, which we all

enjoyed. Before the dance, we walked around and the fellows saw a Gypsy lady telling fortunes. The Gypsy lady told me (ha ha) that a girl with short dark hair was in love with me, but of course you have long, long hair, so I knew it wasn't you. She also said that this girl was standing in a hallway, like a school, and had a book with funny symbols on it. Say, is that chemistry teacher trying to get your attention?

Love to all the family, Dave. DYSLM?

Dear David,

Did I tell you I got my hair cut? Yes, David, I did. And Papa hit the ceiling. His face got so red I thought he was going to explode! Mama, as usual, calmed him down. Now Pauline and Nita want to get their hair cut. Can you just imagine all my sisters with short hair! By the way, I am taking Italian language so I can read the letters from Italy to my mama. And Dave, don't worry about the chemistry teacher. He did ask me out, but I told him I was friends with someone already. Mary was looking over my shoulder when I was reading your letter and asked me what DYSLM meant.

Maggie

(Have you guessed by now what DYSLM means?)

Chapter 11

Bridge Detail

The guys were in the back of the OD truck riding up the mountain. They have been sent to build a bridge over a creek as part of the road they are building. The road had been graded, but no rock had been laid in. In front of them was another truck carrying a load of rock that the men took out of the road (the crew that was breaking up the rocks after the dynamite detail and the crew barring rock).

The men arrived at the mountain creek near the road they are building. They got down from the truck and stood around talking.

"Where are we?"

"In the woods, where do you think?"

"Wake up, smart ass!"

"All out of the truck."

"Now what?"

You got your orders."

"Nobody told us anything, Sarge."

The equipment truck pulled up.

"Arright, step right up, get your tickets to a good meal. Here, take these." He hands equipment to a few men.

"You there, roll up your pants and get into the creek. We have to know how deep it is. (He winks at no one in particular—he knows how deep it is). We gotta form a brigade to set the stones in columns across the creek. Remember, these rocks must support the roadbed to hold up the trucks and machines that go over it, so do your job well. Didn't any of younz get any education about building this here bridge?"

The truck with large heavy stones pulled up and stopped at the edge of the road.

The Sergeant yelled out further orders.

"Arright, you two men here, take the rocks down off the truck and hand them to the men next to you, and you fellows to the men in the creek. Lay them across like you're going to build a bridge. Guffaw, haw haw. These are real blocks you're playing with now, not tinker toys. Come on Muscles, get moving, use your shoulders and back, you're not in school, you're in the ARMY. WE are building a bridge, Buster! Come on, hup, up, hand 'em down, over, over, down into the water! That's it… you got the idea, mister. Now, unload all those blocks, and put them in the correct position. We're building a BRIDGE! And remember, you might just be the one riding over it one day."

Dave was on the bridge detail, and he was also on the relief crew. Other men were cutting down timber to lay across the rocks for the trucks to go over the roadbed.

The roads the men were building were known as *corduroy roads*. They were given this name because they were constructed of cut timber logs stripped of branches which were laid down across a roadbed and thus, were called *corduroy roads*.

(Note: Leonard Parucha, in a letter to the author, gives details of how a bridge was built. See end of this story for details of building bridges. L. Parucha, who was in the CCC, and a writer-historian, had articles about the CCC that were published in Pennsylvania Magazine, and also newspapers.)

Dear Maggie:

Maggie, we built a bridge on the road to White Deer today. Only 17 miles to go.

Dave

Chapter 12

Thanksgiving – Dave is Home on Leave

D ave, how come you're always so quiet? Your letters are so full of questions, but when we are together, you seem like you have nothing to say. I think you mustn't really like me, huh, kid? At least not enough to talk to me," Finished with her speech, Maggie pouted,as she lifted her chin and closed her mouth.

Dave was home on leave, and had an arm around Maggie's shoulder as they sat side by side on the comfortable old couch. He really didn't know how to answer her. He felt so comfortable just sitting beside his beautiful blue-eyed girl. All he wanted to do was to hold her and kiss her and look at her.

"Of course I like you. What makes you say that? You know there's nobody else for me but you."

"In your letters you're always asking me about my girlfriends and my chemistry teacher."

Dave was desperate to get her off those subjects. He just wanted to drink in her warmth and smile, run his fingers through her soft brown hair. He reached up and tucked a stray lock of hair behind her ear. "So tell me about you, sweet darling."

"What do you want to know, David?"

"Ahem, cough, cough. Well, ah, were you born here, on

the North Side?"

"No, David, I wasn't. I was born in New York, in Oswego."

"You surprised me. When did you move here?"

"Well, I was just a little kid when we moved to Pittsburgh. Some cousin or other of my papa's wrote and said Pittsburgh was a better place for us than Oswego, and told my papa that he also could help in his store—he has a small grocery store on East Street."

And there is another reason we moved from New York too, she was thinking of the fright they'd had when the Mafia threatened her dad. But she didn't tell Dave. She'd tell him another time about that—maybe!

She had been told that her dad had a team of matched ponies that pulled a cart with a surrey on top, and the Mafia leader wanted them. Dad would not sell, so the Mafia stole them. But Sam, Margaret's dad, stole them back; and so he was in big trouble with the Mafia because of it.

"So why isn't he working in his cousin's store now?"

Maggie didn't want to go into detail, so she just said, "My papa didn't want to work there anymore. So he got hired at Altman's Feed Store on Suismon Street. They didn't want to hire him at first because he was fifty years old. But my Papa is a strong man so he hung around there and helped people load their trucks and automobiles with one hundred pound sacks of flour and feed. The owner noticed this and finally said, "Sam, do you want to work here for me?" And of course my Papa said yes."

Dave pulled her close. He really didn't want to talk

about her family just now; he just wanted to hold her and plant little kisses up and down her face, her neck, her mouth, and maybe, just maybe, she let him nibble her pretty pink ears. He started to kiss her ears, but she slapped him—hard!

"Stop that, David. Now's not the time for that."

Dave moved over a little and smiled.

Maggie, acting as though nothing had happened said, "So tell me about you, David."

Dave looked sideways at her to see if he could figure out what had just happened between them. Was she playing a game? She had just slapped him, didn't she?

"Well?"

"Well, what?"

"Well, were you born here, or in Timbuktu?"

Dave resigned himself to talking and not kissing. "I was born in Rural Valley."

"I never heard of it. Where is it?"

"Pennsylvania, not too far from Pittsburgh."

"Tell me about it."

"Well, we lived in a small place with my folks and my brothers and sisters."

"Dave, I only know about Millie and Mary. What happened to the others, and where is your papa?"

"Well, my brothers are older than I am, they're all married. And my dad, well, he got sick, and well, he died when I was nine years old."

"Dave, I'm sorry to hear that." Her heart went out to him. "It must have been tough on you and your mom. Is that when you moved to Pittsburgh?"

"Millie moved here when she married Frank, and Mary and Mike—Mike's her husband, lived in Pittsburgh, so my sisters thought it would be best if mom and me moved here too. So, here we are."

"So –"

"Well–"

"Well, this is the most you've ever talked. But I'm sorry to say, it's late, and it's time for you to go, Gypsy."

"Say, Mags, just why do you call me Gypsy. A Gypsy is a woman."

"Where have you been? A Gypsy is a person who travels all over the country, just like you do. And a Gypsy can be either a man or a woman."

"Well, I'm just a travelin' man, not a Gypsy, but if it makes you happy, call me anything you like, just so you love only me, sweetie." Dave kissed her, and heard her papa coming down the stairs. It was late, but he just hated to go. "Maggie, I'll see you tomorrow."

"I have to work a half day tomorrow, Dave."[5]

"But tomorrow's Thanksgiving."

"I have to work a half day, no choice if I want to get paid and not lose my job."

"Well, so long." He did not try to kiss her again.

Chapter 13

Zimmerman Camp, Sugar Valley

The Lost Hunter, December 1934

As the alarm bells sounded, Dave jumped from the narrow cot, quickly pulled on his trousers, and zipped them up. He looked out into the dark night and asked someone what was going on. Getting an answer, and returning to the barracks, he yelled to his partner.

"Git your ass outta that bed, Fergie!"

"Jeez, man, lemme alone. It's the middle of the night!"

Dave jerked the covers off the sleeping man. "Now, dammit—some old guy got himself lost in the woods. We gotta go find him."

Fergie was up in a minute, stretching and yawning. He was tall, lean, and bony, with a strong, square looking jaw, and slight overgrowth of beard. He sat upright on his bunk, rubbing the back of his head.

"Wad'ya say, somebody got lost?" he said sleepily.

All the others were up, rushing to get dressed, and awake.

"I gotta get a shower."

"You don't have time for a shower. Buchanon said there's coffee ready in the mess. C'mon. I'll see you there!" Dave left the barracks.

The snow crunched underfoot. *It's good that there are plenty of trees to keep the wind away. I can hardly see the sky*, the old man thought. *Damn, don't know how I lost him! At least I'm strong and healthy. Never been sick a day in my life!* His thoughts wandered as he tramped through the forest; he was getting hungry. *I sure could go for some hot coffee and a warm fire, or a brandy. A brandy would warm me up!* He thought of the Zimmerman camp, from where he started out. He thought of his nephew, from whom he got separated. He was glad there were no bears around, and all the snakes were hibernating now. *Tarnation*, he thought. *Jennie always said it was my meanness and stubbornness that keeps me going. Well, I guess I am a bit blustery. Tarnation! Where is that boy? Where'd he get off to? Well, if I keep movin', I won't die of cold, just die of starvation! I just know I'll find someone, or they'll find me. North, South, East, West, what direction is best? Tarnation, if I just had a compass. Not that I know what direction I'm heading. There's no sun, can't see any moss. Streams go downhill. I'll go downhill! I'm bound to find something. Maybe one of those CC camps. Can't stop, keep going. Keep going. Keep going.*

In the assembly hall, at one in the morning, the captain spoke to the men. All were seated, drinking hot coffee, trying to look alert after only three to four hours sleep.

"There's an eighty-year-old man out there, walking around, *we hope*, who got separated from his hunting party. His nephew reported him missing, and it's up to us to find him. I don't have to tell you men how cold it is out there. The gentleman has been missing since early yesterday morning. We'll separate into teams, fifteen men in a team, ten teams. Just like the fire rescue teams you were drilled on. All the camps around here are looking for him, but the hunting camp he started out from is nearest to our camp. We are goin' to find him!

"Your sergeant will be the leader of all teams."

The captain walked off the center spot and the sergeant took over, directing the teams and appointing team leaders in less than a minute. The sergeant was very organized and efficient. He assigned stretchers to two of the teams, just in case.

The three buddies, Dave, Fergie, and Frank were on the same rescue team. Fergie was wide awake now as the three chatted.

"Jesus, how did the old guy lose himself?"

"Easy in these woods,Ferg, probably went to piss in private and didn't tell anyone."

"Naw, Dave, he most likely spotted a buck and hid to get a good shot." said Frank.

"Yeah, but aren't they supposed to stay at least two together? asked Fergie."

"Hey Fergie, maybe nobody told the ol' guy. Ha ha!"

"Shut up, Frank, this is serious," said Dave. "You guys wearing two pairs of socks like the cap'n said?"

The two nodded.

"It's a good thing we got heavy boots this year," Dave continued, "not like last year, when they were worn out."

"Yeah, but remember when you didn't have boots at all?"

"Fergie, I remember when I didn't have *shoes*!"

"Yeah, we're lucky we're in this here camp," Frank laughed.

They moved out with the others, donning their caps, zipping up their jackets, and pulling on wool gloves.

Outside, the sergeant gave final orders. "Stay with your assigned group. Each man will be three to four feet from the other; remember, he may have fallen and be covered with snow, so look out for that possibility. You men will have a flare each; only use it if necessary. I've given each leader a revolver. If you find him, alive or dead, fire five shots in succession! All right, men, you have your orders. Move!"

Meanwhile — *Looks like a camp down there. I knew if I'd keep walking I'd find something! Hope they have the coffee pot on. Tarnation, I'd like to freeze to death even with these here long johns.*

Old man walked into the camp and spotted a guard. "Hey you, where is everybody? Inside keeping warm? I need some coffee!"

"Who are you? Where'd you come from? What's your name?"

"I guess I got separated from my hunting partner. I'm

out from the Zimmerman camp, up around here somewhere. My name is Ed, Ed Simon. I need some hot coffee! You got any handy?"

"The whole camp is out lookin' for you. Come on, follow me. There's coffee and a fire in the mess hall."

He fired five shots to let everyone know that the lost hunter has been found. They tramped down the road to the mess hall and went in through the door.*

"You hear that? Five shots. He's found. Sounded like the shots were from the direction of camp."

"You, Ferguson, hightail it down to camp and see where those shots came from. Dave, you go with him. If he's there, tell the guard to fire two more shots. Meanwhile, you men wait just where you are. It may be a false alarm."

Fergie and Dave scrambled down through the woods to camp. No one was around, so Fergie rushed into the mess hall. Dave was right behind him. He spotted the guard, Fletcher, and an old man, whom he assumed was the hunter they were looking for. He spoke to the guard.

"Fletcher, go out and fire two shots to let Serge know the old man is here."

"Who you callin' an old man, you squirt?"

"No offense, mister; we're glad you're okay. Just the whole camp out there is looking for you. More coffee? There's nothing like hot coffee to warm a man up. You hungry … it's just about time for breakfast."

"Yes, I'm hungry! I could eat a stack of flapjacks and more!"

"Some tough old man," Fletch said. "How long was he wandering around, anyway?"

"Almost two days," answered Dave.

"He says he couldn't find his toilet paper, that's why he got lost."

"Come on, make some sense, Frank."

"I'm not kidding, Fergie, he lost his toilet paper, that's what he told me. He said he wound some toilet paper around the branches of trees as he passed them so's he could find his way back, but some joker pulled it off and probably used it, so he lost his markers!"

Everyone had stopped eating breakfast to listen. At this point they all started to laugh, some to the point of losing half their food out of their mouths. One guy had just taken a mouthful of coffee and spit it out all over the guy across from him.

The cook, Bill, came in at this point to see what all the commotion was about.

"Hey, Bill, this stuff you pushed around in the kitchen is pretty damn good! The last cook made pure puke."

"Don't butter him up, Snake, or you'll spoil the guy. Bill will think you mean it!"

"Yeah, maybe he took the toilet paper for us since, you notice, we got prunes today for starters!"

"Shaddup, youse guys, or tomorrow I'll give youse a double dose of prunes!"

He went back into the kitchen. Bill looked at the menu for tomorrow. He held a wooden spoon in his right hand

while perusing the menu. "I'll get those guys yet."

Breakfast included a bacon omelet, French fried potatoes, cereal, stewed prunes, bread and butter, and milk and coffee.

Chapter 14

Christmas

*I*nside Maggie's house, on the North Side of Pittsburgh, she recounted her letter to Dave, in which she asked, "Did you go to Christmas Mass?" His reply had read, "Yes, I went to Church services on Christmas."

He then went on to tell her about his guarding the fires at night to keep warm, and what they do in winter to keep busy, such as go to their library, and school, and such.

Dave writes Maggie that Christmas services weren't so bad after all. He is also taking classes at camp, such as compulsory first aid on Monday nights. And, they teach classes in forestry, electricity, and machinery, as well.

He writes to Maggie in French that he loves her and asks if she's still his girl. When does she want to get married?

After electricity class, Dave left with his buddy, Frank. While the two walked through the cold night Dave asked, "Who pulled guard tonight, Frank?"

"Fergie. When are you on duty, Dave?"

"Over the weekend. I asked for leave, but I didn't get it. How 'bout you?"

"I pulled guard on this weekend too."

"Yeah, Dave. Isn't it funny, we both lived on the North Side and I didn't know you till we came here?"

"Yeah, Frank. But the North Side is a pretty big place."

"Well, I mean somewhere, like Isaly's, or on the main street, you know."

Dave didn't think that warranted a response. They continued walking to the barracks, where it was a lot warmer inside.

Jim Koch was the company clerk. He remembered the incident of the lost hunter. I have a copy of a newspaper in which this is recorded. Mrs. J. Zimmerman, Lock Haven, PA sent the newspaper article with picture.

Chapter 15
January 1935

Guard Duty

*T*he night was still and dark. Somewhere in the forest surrounding the camp, a wolf howled. Dave and Frank stepped out of their barracks into the cold, frigid night air. The snow crunched underfoot. They are on guard duty, required to watch that the fires around the camp and in the mess hall keep burning. He and Frank are walking side by side, making the rounds.

The mess hall is located at the edge of the camp. It is dark because of the nearness of the huge pines. They discover that the embers in the fireplace in the mess hall have all but gone out.

"Christ, Frank, how the hell are we supposed to fix the damn fire when we can't even see in front of our face!" exploded Dave.

"Calm down, buddy. Jeez, no one who knows you as a quiet kid would ever suspect you had such an explosive temper!" replied Frank. "Here, light a match, kid."

Dave pulled off his knitted wool cap, and shoved his hair back, which had sprung down over his forehead. He stepped back. Frank struck a match that went up in a quick flare and cupped it in his hand. They were in the mess hall, trying to get the fire lit.

"Here, Dave, over here."

They walked the few steps over and began building the fire, and of course, the tiny light from the match went out.

"Shit, it almost burnt my finger!" said Frank. He lit another match. "Here, Dave, light this crushed paper; it ought to start up quick with this here tinder around it. Then we can toss on some kindling." There were already logs in the fireplace.

Finally, they got the fire burning. Dave visibly started to relax a little and let out a big breath.

"Say, what's botherin' you, buddy?" asked Frank. "I know when you've got something on your mind! I don't like to pry, but you're not acting like the Dave I know."

Dave looked sideways at Frank and looked at the ground in front of him as they started walking again. He is thinking about what Frank said. In his usual fashion, he cleared his throat, and said, "You're right, I don't like to talk about personal things, but, I have to admit, I'm worried about something Maggie wrote me in one of her letters. She is going to night school and there's a teacher there, she says who likes her. He asked her out. That worries me."

"Well, I don't know your girl, Dave. I've never met her, but from all the letters she sends you, and the magazines, I don't think you have to worry so much."

Dave cleard his throat again, looks at Frank sideways. He says, "Yeah, it's not her so much, but that chemistry teacher that worries me. We're a long way from home, Frank. I'm sure she misses me, but what if she gets lonely and does go out with him. She might find out she likes him better than me."

"Didn't you ask her to marry you? What did she say?"

"Ahh, ahh, I'd rather not say."

"What? Did she say no?"

"No."

"Then what?"

"She says she don't want to get married for at least three more years."

"Oh."

Chapter 16
The Bedspread

January 1935
Dear Dave,

I have spent the past few days at my sister Angeline's house. She is teaching me to crochet a bedspread. Now don't get any ideas, David. For I still don't want to get married for a few more years. But know this, that I love you, darling, dearly.

David, I feel so bad. Angeline won't talk about it, and I know you won't either, but she has had another bad time, losing her pregnancy. I think it was only a two months baby. She wants a child badly, but I guess God had other plans. Personally, I think it is the tight corsets she wears. You couldn't pay me to wear one of them. I guess it was the old-fashioned Gibson Girl look that she was wanting, but did not think wearing that old tight thing had anything to do with what happened.

By the way, how many children do you want, David? You do want children, don't you, dear? I surely hope so. I do.

Love, and plenty of hugs, and please don't show this letter to any of your buddies.

Your pal, Maggie

Winter Thoughts — City of Pittsburgh

It was freezing cold walking home from the streetcar stop. Maggie huddled inside her warm brown wool coat. Pauline, taller than Maggie, but just as slim, walked beside her sister. Both wore scarves and hats to guard against the cold. After being at work all day, they were pouring out thoughts they had carried with them all day long and couldn't express while on the job.

"I heard Dad talking about buying a farm," said Maggie.

"I don't think we can afford it. You must have heard wrong," replied Pauline.

"No, I didn't. He wants to grow vegetables to sell and get some cows for milk, and get some chickens and horses too. I heard him and Mama talking when I went down to turn off the lights last night."

Suddenly, Maggie changed the subject.

"Pauline, what do you think of David?"

"He's a nice enough boy."

Maggie felt confused. She was a little unsure of Dave's intentions, and at the same time, she knew that he wanted her. *Maybe,* she thought, *I'm just unsure of myself and what I want. Do I know what my feelings are? Mama and Papa want me to marry an Italian, Catholic boy. Dave is neither. But they do like him. He is also younger than me.*

She told Pauline about her feelings, how she feels about Dave, and what she knows her parents want and expect of her. She also told her about feeling responsible to help earn money for her family, as it is the Depression and things are tough.

"Pauline, I think I really do love him. Mama and Papa like him, though he isn't Italian. What do you think? He said he would try to go to the Catholic Mass up there in the CCC camp. I know he would do anything for me."

"Honey, wait and see if he gets a job when he comes home from camp. You know how bad things are right now. And you've seen the headlines in the newspaper with talk of war. It's scary. And I don't think his mama hardly has any money. She can't work. She just lives on what Dave sends her home, doesn't she?"

"Paulie, I think she gets a check from the camp, because Dave said they send home twenty-five dollars a month. He only gets to keep five dollars."

"Maybe he can get a job with Conroy and Prugh. They always need someone. Glass is always needed, you know."

"And there's Fort Pitt Bedding down at the river."

"I think I'll drop in on Dave's mama tomorrow. After all, it's Saturday. At least I don't have to work at Conroy's tomorrow."

The winter days went crawling slowly by. February and March passed uneventfully for both Dave and Maggie. Dave had his everyday routine up at camp in the forest, and Maggie had her everyday routine back on Pittsburgh's North Side.

Dave got up at the crack of dawn each day in the quiet winter of a forest, his every waking thought of Maggie, as he followed camp routine, doing his daily tasks, and going to required classes. In his leisure time on the weekends, like everyone else in camp, the fellows gathered for a movie, or the occasional entertainment of a live vaudeville act in the assembly or mess hall. At Maggie's request, on a Sunday, he would attend a Catholic Mass. If he or any of his buddies got a pass for a day, they would go to a nearby town, like Watsontown, or Lock Haven, to enjoy themselves for a time. There was not much to do in the winter in camp except kitchen duty, guard duty, or cleanup, and of course, attend classes, or spend time at the small camp library. He wrote frequently to Maggie, anxious to see her again. Now and then, the Tea Springs camp was invited to another camp, such as Pine camp, or Ole Bull, to enjoy something special like a boxing match, or the appearance of a movie star or someone from vaudeville, or a singer. The federal government, mainly through the efforts of Franklin Delano Roosevelt, tried to keep everyone working.

Finally, March appeared on the scene, bringing with it a stinging wind, but with lots of hope for the days ahead. Dave was lucky enough to acquire a three-day pass to get back home to Pittsburgh and his beloved Maggie.

Dave surprised Maggie by waiting for her after work. As she came down the cement steps of Conroy & Prugh, on Western Avenue, where she worked, a smile lit up her face. Maggie stopped in her tracks as Dave sauntered up to her. "Surprise," he said.

"David, when did you get back?"

He placed his hands on her shoulders and kissed her soundly on the lips.

"Just now."

They started walking hand in hand as Pauline caught up to them.

"Hello, David. How are you? It's good to see you again." Then she slowed her steps and hung just behind them as they all walked.

"Maggie, do you have to go right home?" Dave asked. "Could you stop by my house?"

"David, yes. If I don't go home first, Mama will worry. Why don't you come home with me now and have supper with us? The family would be happy to see you."

"I'd better see my mother and let her know I'm back. I haven't been home yet. I came right over to see you as soon as I got off the train. If I can't make it for supper, I'll walk over later tonight."

He left her and Pauline at the corner where he turned off to go home. They waved as he ran up the alleyway to his house.

Later, at home Maggie asked her older brother, "Phil, what is love?"

"Why, Maggie, did you see a Rudolph Valentino movie again?"

"Be serious, what is love? Have you ever thought about it?"

"Yeah, Sis, I have, and ya know, I think it's a feeling, a tickling feeling around the heart that can't be touched."

Just before Dave had to return to camp, he and Maggie spent some time together at his house. Dave wanted to kiss Maggie, but was afraid she would balk at his advances. He did not know when he would see her again. He also knew he should let her leave, but he kept talking while they were sitting at the kitchen table in order to keep her with him longer. He was gathering courage to kiss her while he was talking. She could see by the way he was looking at her that he wanted to kiss her. At last he reached across the table and grasped her hand. "Dave, it's getting late." Maggie said, " I have to go." She stood up to leave and he hurried around the table and reached for her, intending to kiss her. But Maggie turned her head, knowing that if she let him, she would have a hard time dragging herself away.

The more she resisted, the more he persisted. Finally Maggie got mad, took off the ring, and thrust it at him. "Don't think you can take liberties with me just because you gave me a ring!"

With that, she walked out the door, slamming it behind her. Dave paced the floor, thinking. He had to leave early in the morning to go back to camp. Later as he drifted off to sleep, he thought about what he would write to Maggie. She meant the world to him; he could not lose her because of his hasty impulses.

Dave wrote this letter to Maggie just before returning to CCC camp. On opening the front door, Maggie found a letter addressed to her:

Dear Maggie,

I'm sorry for detaining you when you wanted to leave. It was my foolishness and I don't know why I did it. I should have known better. I hope you will forgive me, for I'm certainly sorry that this had to happen on the night I'm to leave. Will you accept the ring back? You know I really love you and can't do without you. I always seem to argue with you, and I ask your forgiveness.

Love, Dave

Then, back at camp.

Loganton, PA

"Hello, sweetheart, do you still love me? We made pretty good time until we reached Lock Haven, then we had to lay over for about three hours. We got in about 4:30 A.M., and it was just about zero degrees out. The place sure looks different and I'm really lonely without you. I wish I was back in Pittsburgh. I'm glad you have forgiven me, and it makes me love you all the more. Most girls would have quit me after what I did. I don't know what I would do without you, because I love you so much. Gee, sweetheart, I didn't know you were in earnest when you said you wanted to go home, but let's forget it. Let me know if you still love me as

ever, as I love you. I have to close, as I don't want the captain to find me writing instead of working. I close, longing to be near you.

My regards to all.

Love, Dave

Springtime at Camp
April, Loganton, PA

Hello, darling,

How's my sweetheart? Several men left camp Sunday, and it sure is lonely up here, it makes you feel lost. Forty men left and fifteen out of the barracks I'm in, including the guy that had the bunk next to me. There are only twenty left.

Well, sweet, I may be home sooner than you expect, as Pennsylvania doesn't seem to want to help finance the CCC in the next two years.

I guess I have to stand it a while longer, though I would rather be with you. I hope time flies so I can see you soon again, as I'm lonely without you, dear.

Well, I suppose you're listening to Joe Penner[7] while I'm writing, as I'm also listening to him.

Sweetheart, I close, loving you always.

Love, Dave

In the spring, Dave got leave to go home for Easter. Meanwhile, Maggie's parents had bought a farm near Mars,

Pennsylvania, just about an hour and a half from Pittsburgh. On the day that Dave came home, Maggie and her brother Phil were working at the farm with their father. The rest of the family was at home on Lovett Way. When Maggie's sister Annie got the mail that morning, she was excited to see that Maggie had received a letter from David.

"Look Nita," said Annie, Maggie will be happy to get this letter from David!"

"Let's see," said Nita.

Nita had a car and was the only one in the family, besides their Papa, who knew how to drive. She had planned to go out to the farm that day.

"Mama, I'm going out to the farm. Do you want to go?"

"No, not today. I'm in the middle of baking my bread. Take Annie with you."

Annie was thrilled that she was going in the new car with her big sister. And both girls were happy to bring Maggie her letter from Dave. But just as they were pulling away from the house, a young man came running toward them, flagging them down. It was David! He had hitched a ride from the train station to Maggie's house. When the sisters told him where they were going, Dave jumped into the car and the three headed off to surprise Maggie.

Maggie was in the field planting cold weather crops with Phil. The two were having a race to see who gets to the end of the row first.

When the car pulled up, Annie jumped out and ran to Maggie shouting, "Maggie, Maggie look! See what came in the mail for you!"

Maggie straightened up, and pushed her hair away from her face. "What's all the shouting, little sister?"

Annie handed Maggie the letter. A smile lit up her face as she took it. David waited only until he saw Maggie begin to read the letter before sneaking up behind her.

When Maggie turned and saw him she screamed, "Dave, Dave, you stinker!"

She threw herself in his arms just as her Papa came walking out of the chicken coop.

"What's going on?" he shouted.

He looked out into the field and saw Dave and Maggie embracing.

Mr. Rossi was not a tolerant man and did not like anyone, especially a man, taking advantage of his daughters. After all, he had to protect them and besides, Maggie was working—planting.

Phil knew his dad and what he was thinking.

"Dad, it's just Dave," said Phil. He just got here. He's probably on leave from camp."

Mr. Rossi knew that Dave was respectful of his strict rules, and that he would not do anything to hurt his Maggie or disrespect the family.

Meanwhile, Maggie was so happy to see Dave.

"What's going on?" Dave said as a way of greeting.

"What do you think?" answered Maggie, showing him her dirty hands.

"I only have today, sweetheart. I have to go back tomorrow."

Hand in hand, they walked back to the farmhouse.

"I don't like farming," Maggie told Dave. "It's too much

work. I hope you won't want to live on a farm, David."

"No danger of that."

Back at Camp

RD-1, Loganton, PA
April 16, 1935

Hello, adorable,

How's my sweet since I've been back at camp? Gee, honey, when I arrived at camp, I wished I was back in Pgh. again.

Believe me, we're having a blizzard up here; it's blowing and snowing and sure is cold.

No rookies have come in, but I hope they do soon.

Well, honey, I hope you have forgiven me for my foolishness. I'm really sorry for making you sore at me. It was heaven being with you for a while, really it was, but it was too short a stay to suit me.

Honey, I would like to talk about a lot of things with you, but it's impossible to at your home. What I mean is a heart to heart talk.

I know you want to marry me, and the same for me. I realize we can't get married till I have a job, and it's sweet of you to wait for me. I couldn't get along without you. I really only quarrel in fun and don't mean anything by it. I guess I'm just a darn fool and should know better.

Write soon, as I need your letter for consolation.
My deepest love for such a beautiful girl as you.

Dave
Loganton, PA
April 1935

Hello adorable,
You seem worried that we might get put into an army to fight, but don't worry about that; they can't put us into the army without giving us a discharge from the CCC and sending us home.
Anyway, if they would take us, what's the difference; plenty others have gone before and came back. Maybe you are preaching to me, honey, but I really don't blame you. It shows that you really love me and want me.
Gee, sweetheart, I hope you don't stay mad at me for signing up again and I hope you love me as I love you.
Well, there's only three fellows in the barracks I'm in. The captain put the rest in the other barracks. We sure have plenty of room to ourselves, but it's kind of lonely.
With nothing more to say, I close, loving you for always.

Love,
Dave

Loganton, PA
May 1935

Hello, sweetheart,
How's my beautiful getting along anyway?
Well, it's been a pretty good week. We are doing quite a bit of whitewashing lately and it's pretty easy.

All the fellows had their picture taken in a group on Wednesday and it was brought back on Thursday, but I didn't get to see it. We'll probably get soaked a buck if we want one. They are supposed to take an aerial picture also. I hope it comes out good. We're still fixing up the camp.

There's not much to do these days. So we mostly play baseball and go swimming.

Well, sweetheart, I sure wish I was in that car with you coming from the farm with your head on my shoulder. I sure do love you, honey, no fooling. I wish I was with you now.

Love always, Dave

Summer — Loganton, PA
Camp S-114

June 3, 1935

Hello, sweetheart,
I finally received a letter from you. I didn't write because I was waiting for a letter from you, which I finally received. I thought you may have forgotten me, but I guess you didn't.

Saturday before last I went to New Columbia with one of the fellows who is from Philadelphia. He knew some people there, and we had a good time. Last Saturday I went to Williamsport and didn't get back till after midnight. I may go up to Slate Run Camp about two weeks from now; all Pittsburgh fellows up there.

You know Harold Miller, he's up there also.

I was invited to go to Philadelphia for the Fourth of July, but I don't think I'll go.

I sure miss your letters, and you, and I certainly love you, honey.

Loving you always,
Dave

RD-1, Loganton, PA
Camp S-114
6-17-35

Hello, honey,

How's tricks going along anyway? Anything new in the old 'Burgh? It's tough to be away, no fooling. Well, I don't have long in this army anymore, a little over three months.

What have you been doing with all of your spare time? Have you finished that bedspread yet?

We have a new hobby up here now and that's collecting different species of butterflies and moths.

Has your Dad got any tigers or lions on his farm? I thought maybe he had. He has quite a few animals, doesn't he? Horses, cows, chickens, and you say a few sheep? And

I remember you told me the cat had kittens.

Well, it's Sunday and it's kind of late. I think I'll close, girl of my dreams.

Love, always,
  Dave

Loganton, PA
7-15-35

Hello, honey,

I hope you don't mind this short letter this time, and I'll tell you the reason for it. Two of us fellows decided to go swimming at a dam the CCC's made. Well it was ten miles one way and ten back, and we had to walk, and I'm so tired I don't feel like writing much. Anyway, we had a good time, even though we're tired out. We had to work last Saturday.

Gee, kid, I'm sure tired of this place, no fooling. It's getting on my nerves and I'll be glad when I get out; it's worse up here than it ever was.

I suppose you were at the farm Sunday, as usual, and no doubt you're tired of it as I am of this place.

Still love me, honey? I sure miss you and can't wait till I see you again. You certainly mean a lot to me, honey, more than you'll ever know.

I hope you don't get tired of my talking of love to you, or do you? I close, loving you as much as a fellow can love a girl.

Dave

825 Lovett Way N.S.
Pgh., Pa.
7-18-35

Hi, honey,

How's trix? Glad you enjoyed your swim Sunday. Only I think it would have been much better if you wouldn't have walked so much.

Anna Onderka was asking about you. She seemed very sorry that she didn't get to see you when you were home. She sure has a case on you, kid, and I don't mean maybe.

David, I heard you were mean and grouchy when you got up from bed to catch your train when you left for camp. You hurt your mother's feelings terrible. You didn't mean to be like that, did you, sweetheart? I kinda wish you were home now, honey, and that your time would be up so you could be near me always.

I forgot to tell you that Christina was asking about you too. Tell me, David, just what did you do to get my girlfriends to make them love you so? Send me the formula so I can try it on a dear friend of mine.

Gee, honey, I'm stuck trying to figure out what to write. So I'll say I love you, man of my dreams. Perhaps not as much as I could, yet time usually makes one's love grow stronger.

Regards from all.

Love, Maggie (12:35 A.M.)

825 Lovett Way, N.S.
Pgh. Pa
7-21-35

Hello Darling,

How's my honey? I just came from the country, David, and I can say that I really enjoyed myself today.

There were about 25 or 30 people out there today. Phillip and my dad hung a large, thick rope on a tree limb and made a swing. Boy, it sure was fun swinging on it.

Pauline, my girlfriend, and I went for a long walk on the road and saw a large black snake. It was about as long as the snakeskin you brought home. It's a good thing the darn thing was dead, or we would have been scared stiff.

Gee, darling, I started this letter late and can hardly believe it's so late. So I will close loving you.

Maggie (12:45 A.M.)

August at Tea Springs

Camp S-114, Loganton, PA

Hello Honey,

How's my sweetheart? Not working too hard, I hope. There's nothing much to do up here these days. Some of the

fellows and I were wrestling and it was so hot, we took showers afterward. Do you know how cold the water is here in the mountains? Well, it was like pouring ice down our backs, no fooling.

Well, kid, we are going to see a vaudeville show tonight. I hope it's a good one.

I saw a movie last weekend. It was called "It Happened One Night."

Well, having nothing else to say. I close, loving you always.

Regards to all the family.

Dave

It was late August at camp. Dave and a few of his friends were lounging on some large rocks enjoying the fine weather when Dave got an idea. He had been staring at the back of the plain white t-shirt one young man was wearing when he thought it might be interesting to draw something on it.

Before long, one of the other guys noticed what Dave was doing and went over to have a look.

"Whatcher doin'?"

"What's it look like?"

Stepping closer to get a better look, he saw that Dave was drawing a beautiful girl on the back of the shirt.

"Hey, yer good. Would ya do one fer me, Dave, huh?"

Without looking up, Dave said, "Yeah, for a quarter."

"How 'bout a dime?"

"Yeah, okay."

The guy who was wearing the shirt pulled it off and took long look at the picture Dave drew.

It was a girl in a swimsuit sitting with her arms clasping her knees, wearing a large sun hat that covered most of her face.

"Hey, Dave, is this your girl?"

Dave's face reddened, as he envisioned Maggie in a swimsuit. He answered gruffly, "No." Then he said to the man waiting, "Your turn."

The fellow sat down.

"Hold still, don't move," Dave told him as he began sketching again. This time it was a scene of a mountain and a pine tree. When Dave was finished, the fellow looked at the picture in surprise.

"Hey, how come ya didn't do a picher of a girl? I ain't payin' you no dime fer no mountain!"

Dave didn't respond but stomped off in anger. He went into his barracks and sat on his bunk. He missed Maggie something fierce. He pulled out a piece of stationary and began writing to her.

August, 1935
Dear Maggie,

There is nothing to do here today. It is Sunday and we don't work on Sunday. I drew some pictures on jerseys for some fellows.

I can't wait to see you again and hold you in my arms. Best regards to all the family and your girlfriends.

Love, Dave

Chapter 17
Coming Home for Good

⌒

*J*he time was coming for Dave to make a decision about continuing with the Conservation Corps or going home. On the one hand, he liked the steady income, and didn't mind camp life—the food was good and he had come to enjoy working in the fresh mountain air. But when he thought about his sweet Maggie, he, of course, wanted to be near her. The problem was that the job situation in Pittsburgh was still not good. In August he sent Maggie this short post card.

August 1935
Loganton, PA
Camp S-114

Dear Maggie,
I am thinking of signing up again.

As ever, Dave

Maggie didn't mince words when she replied to Dave's message.

Sept. 20, 1935

Well, David, I might as well get to the point, as I see there's no use of beating around the bush. I understand you wish to sign up again. Just do as you please, as you have your own life to live, but just in case you do sign up again, I want you to forget you ever knew me.

I guess this is all I have to say.

I close, your friend.

Maggie
(Let me know your intentions in the next letter.)

Dave was more than a little shocked by Maggie's ultimatum. *I want you to forget you ever knew me* stunned him. He wasted no time in responding.

Loganton, PA
9-26-35

Hello Maggie,

I'll be home Monday evening at eight o'clock or Tuesday morning at twelve thirty, I don't know which.

We're having a last big inspection Friday morning.

I'm going to see if I can't get a live black snake to bring home. I'll be seeing you soon.

Dave

Chapter 18
Returning Home

September 1935

Maggie and Mrs. Bell took the trolley from the North Side, across the river to Grant Street and walked the rest of the way to the train station. Pennsylvania Union Station looked deceiving as the young woman and the older woman climbed the slight rise of cobblestones. Circular stone walls, as high as Maggie's shoulders, greeted them like open arms, as though urging them to enter the center doors. Overhead in the vestibule was a glass domed Victorian roof. Thetwo women walked through the archway where glass-paned doors on either side of an expanse of dark stone wall confronted them. As they entered they found themselves in a massive, high-ceilinged hall. There were solid oak doors on the left, and tall arched windows on the right. There were brass-barred ticket windows, where lines of people were buying tickets.

Maggie looked around, noticing the polished oak benches lined up like church pews. She'd better have Dave's mother sit down while she looked for Dave. Mrs. Bell, dressed in her Sunday best with her brimmed hat, decorated with a flower, had clearly been taxed by the walk from the streetcar. But she was anxious to see her son and

Maggie had to convince her to to sit and rest. Once she got her settled on a bench, Maggie proceeded through the large room to the doors at the far end. A sense of excitement carried her along as the brisk air greeted her when she pushed through the final door to the platform. There were several idle passenger cars on the tracks. Steam clouds enveloped her as people hurried by in the din. Maggie looked around for Dave. Maybe his train had not yet arrived.

Suddenly a huge black steam locomotive blew an ear-splitting whistle and began to slow down as it entered the depot. Dave stood in the aisle of the swaying car, trying to retrieve his duffel bag without losing his balance. As he reached up over the seats, he glanced out the narrow windows at the smoky city. Pittsburgh hadn't changed. It was still the same grimy city. But it felt good to be back in the old 'Burgh.

Before stepping down from the train, Dave stopped momentarily on the top step and looked for Maggie, but with so many people swarming around, it was hard to see if she was here. He descended the steps and put his duffel bag on the ground, securing it between his brown leather shoes, as he stopped to light a Camel.

Maggie stood on the train platform; her heart thudding with excitement. She stood on tiptoe and stretched her neck trying to see above and around the milling crowd. A tall man in a crumpled suit nearly toppled her as he rushed hurriedly past.

At last, Maggie glimpsed Dave. Clutching her handbag to her chest, she ran toward him and just as suddenly stopped. She thought her heart would burst in her chest, as she had become overwhelmed at the very sight of him. They hadn't been together all summer. Dave hadn't changed a bit. He stood there, head bent, lighting a cigarette. Lifting her chin a notch, in an effort to calm down, and taking a deep breath, Maggie walked toward him.

Dave lifted his head after lighting his cigarette. A smile erupted from deep inside and planted itself on his face as he spotted Maggie. She was wearing her perky little green velvet hat perched forward, nearly on her forehead. He couldn't stop staring. He was riveted to the spot at the unexpected sight of her. His muscles wouldn't work. He felt like an idiot, just staring at her. At last he came to his senses and carelessly tossed his cigarette away, taking Maggie in his arms. The sharp corner of her handbag dug into his chest as he hugged her tightly. They stood there for some time just drinking in the sight of each other. They ignored the people bustling by, the sounds of the train, the clanking of the couplings between the cars. They were unaware of the steam swirling around the huge black oiled wheels beside them.

"Step back, step back please," shouted the conductor. He broke the spell.

"You're a sight for sore eyes, kid."

Maggie stepped back out of Dave's embrace to get a better look at him. Pleasure and joy filled her. Her eyes widened with excitement and she smiled from ear to ear. It had been too long. Her heart swelled with fullness!

Inside the station, Mrs. Bell was growing anxious and

started walking toward the platform. When she saw Dave and Maggie approach, she hurried forward and put her arms around her youngest son. She couldn't speak. She kissed him and smiled. She was thrilled to have him back. "Son, son," she said, as she wiped the tears from her eyes. "I'm glad you're back. Let's go home!"

"Mom," he said, as he wrapped his arms around her shoulders affectionately and squeezed.

The three walked from the Pittsburgh Union Station to the world outside of the terminal.

"Well kid, do we walk or grab a trolley?" Maggie smiled.

She thought back to the time when he left two years ago to go to work in the Pennsylvania National Forest at Bald Eagle Mountain, for the CCC. He had been so far away from her. She had really missed him, despite the fact that she tried to hide it from him sometimes and herself too. She got tired of him being a faraway lover. She didn't know what she would have done if he had chosen not to come home. She had always been afraid that he would fall in love with someone else. After all, she did hear that girls did sometimes visit the camp; although he had assured her that he only loved her and no one else.

"Dave," Maggie said as they navigated the busy streets, "I was just thinking. You can't imagine how I felt when I read your last postcard. You know … the one where you said you were coming home? I'm just so glad you're back, sweetheart. I missed you so."

Dave and Maggie were so engrossed in each other that they almost forgot that Dave's mom was with them. Mrs.

Bell was puffing and having a hard time keeping up with them. When they reached the corner at Sixth Street she offered, "Let's stop in Woolworth's and get some ice cream. I would just like to sit down for a bit."

"Your wish is my command, Mom," said Dave with an exaggerated bow.

Mrs. Bell was a frugal woman who had had a hard life but ice cream was one of her great loves.

As the three sat down at the counter at Woolworth's, Maggie suggested, "Maybe we should take the trolley the rest of the way home, David, your mother can't walk much further."

"Oh, I'm fine, kids. Ice cream always makes me feel better," Mrs. Bell joked.

" Do they still charge a dime for a trolley ride?"

"Dave, you haven't been gone that long! Yes, they do, but I did buy three tokens for a quarter on our way to meet you. We'll have to go back to Wilkens Jewelers to the streetcar stop."

"Okay by me. Maggie. By the way, Charlie says hello. He came up to camp to see me just before I left. The kid hitchhiked all the way."

"How is your cousin, Dave? Why did he go up to camp? He isn't eligible, is he?"

"Naw, he can't join. He just wishes he could. His dad makes too much money for him to join the CCC. Right Mom?"

"That's true, Davey."

"Oh, I wanted to tell you both that my mother is making a special spaghetti dinner in your honor tonight, dear and

my parents are hoping you'll both be able to come."

"We'll be there, Maggie. Right, Mom?   My mother loves your mom's cooking."

Mrs. Bell smiled shyly. "Tell your mother that I thank her for the kind invitation."

After a delicious dinner at Maggie's house, Dave and Maggie went for a walk down the main street. David took her by the arm and they stopped in front of a jewelry store to look at the rings. They looked at each other, and then back to the rings.

"Marry me, Maggie. Marry me now, this minute, tomorrow. I don't want to wait three years."

"Oh, David. You know we have to save up for all of this. Besides, we have to apply for the license and set a date!"

"Dave, Conroy's is hiring. Go with us on Monday and I'm sure they'll hire you."

"So, when do you want to get married, Maggie? When?" He pressed her for an answer.

"After you get your job, we'll set a date for..." she looked at him shyly, "for our wedding."

Now at least he had an answer. He knew her feelings. He knew they had to wait until there was enough money, until he got a job. And of course, they both wanted a fairly decent wedding with her family and his. There was the matter of arrangements, best man, maid of honor, and so on. There was too much to think about. But he didn't want to think, he wanted to get married... now. Oh well, what could he do but wait, and dream dreams.

Civilian life was an adjustment. The first day back home, Dave felt good just to be at home. That night, in his own bed, it felt good just to lie there. The next morning he enjoyed not having to jump out of bed and hustle into a cold shower with a bunch of other guys. He stretched his arms above his head, swung out of bed, and reached for a cigarette. As he breathed out the first long drag, he thought of Maggie and her happy smile upon seeing him at the station. Man, it felt good holding her in his arms again.

As he looped the short sleeves of a white t-shirt through his hands and pulled it down over his head and down his tanned chest, the image of the camp and the forest came to him. He pictured the beautiful bright sunrises and trekking up the wooded mountain trails with Frank to get to their jobs. The thought of a *job* jolted him to the present. Today he had to look for one. Maggie had said there were lots of jobs to be had at Conroy and Prugh Glass. He'd decided he better hustle!

His mom was in the kitchen. There was a pot of coffee on the stove. He poured himself a cup, put in two spoons of sugar, and poured in thick, yellow creamy milk from the Wilson's Evaporated Milk can. This was certainly a change from the pitchers of fresh milk and cream on the tables at the camp mess.

"Good coffee, Mom." He lit another cigarette. "I'm going over to Conroy's today to see about getting a job. Maggie said they're hiring.

Chapter 19
A Job for Dave

Dave accompanied Maggie and her sisters Nita and Pauline to work.

"This is the office, Dave," Maggie explained as they entered.

"Mr. Wisneski, I'd like you to meet David Bell."
David looked directly at Sigmund Wisneski and shook his outstretched hand with a good grip.

Sigmund Wisneski did not offer Dave a chair.

"I'm looking for work," said Dave.

"You've come to the right place. Fill out this form and bring it back tomorrow. You can start right now. The wage is twenty-eight cents per hour. Follow me." he said. And without a glance back at Maggie, Dave left the office with Mr. Wisneski.

After a tour of the plant they entered the *red room*, where Mr. Wisneski explained, "This is where we buff the scratches out of the glass before they go down to the silvering room. All the marks have to be gone to make a good quality mirror." He showed Dave all the equipment and pointed out the heavy canvas aprons hanging on the wall. "You can wear one of these to keep the red rouge from getting on your clothes. Lunch break is twelve noon." He said and abruptly left.

Dave watched the others for a few minutes. There were only a few men working. A tall thin man walked over. "I'm George. I'll show you the ropes."

Dave donned an apron and took a spot at the blocking machine table and started in with the *red stuff*. At 3:30, he was ready to go home.

This certainly was different than working in the forest, but better than barring rock and getting your toes smashed. At lunch that day, he told Maggie he would see her at home, since his shift ended at 3:30 and hers an hour later.

"Next week I'll be doing nine and a half hours like you

"So how do you like being a regular workingman, David? Is it too much for you after having your freedom in the forest?" Maggie teased.

He ignored her remark. "Think of it this way," he said. "Maybe my working hard will get you a big diamond ring some day."

She just smiled at him and turned to go back inside with the other girls.

At her house the following Saturday, Maggie tried on her beautiful "blue diamond" glass earrings. When she wore these, she thought of herself as a movie star—a real beauty. She raised her hair with her left hand, looked this way and that in the old spotted mirror above the kitchen sink, daydreaming about Dave and what he might say when he saw her in her new dangling earrings and new hairstyle.

I know, she thought, *I'll borrow Anna Onderka's fake fur neck piece too!*

"Ta ta," interrupted her older sister, "what're you getting all gussied up for? Going on a date?"

She ignored her sister Nita and called out to Pauline.

"Pauline, would you go with me to Carlisle's?"

"Maggie! Did Dave finally pop the question?"

"He asked me to marry him again, for the umpteenth time, and I finally agreed."

"Did you set a date?"

"I told him sometime next year."

"Then why do you want to go to Carlisle's so soon?"

"Just dreaming. It is exciting. I guess I should find out how much the gowns cost, so I can save up."

Secretly, in her heart, she wished she did not have to wait a year. But at least she could go and try on the gowns and see what she liked.

"So, you're not going out with Dave, then?"

"Not now. I just want to try on some gowns. Would you go with me?"

The two sisters walked down the street and crossed busy East Ohio Street to Carlisle's wedding gown shop. It was an old shop, having been there since 1889. A pleasant saleswoman greeted them. "May I help you?"

"Yes, we'd like to try on some gowns."

"Both of you?"

Maggie and Pauline looked at each other and laughed. "No, just her." Pauline tilted her head toward Maggie.

"I'm assuming you want to try on a wedding gown?"

"Yes."

"Are you planning on getting married soon?"

"We haven't set an exact date yet," said Maggie.

The saleswoman showed them to the racks and racks of beautiful white gowns. "We have quite a few to choose from. Did you have anything particular in mind? Satin? Silk? Voile? Taffeta? Lace? And you look to be a size six. What size are you?"

Maggie looked at Pauline. She was used to making all her dresses and had bought very few in the last couple of years. She didn't want the woman to think she was ignorant of her own size. "I've lost a few pounds, so I really don't know."

"Nerves, yes? Here we are." The saleswoman took a gown off the rack. "This is about your size. Do you like it?"

"Not quite. It's too fussy." Maggie thought a plain satin would be cheaper. She looked at the section that held her assumed size and pointed at a plain satin gown. "I'd like to try on this one."

Though Maggie didn't know it, Pauline was secretly looking at the gowns too. She had just met a boy named Stanley at a friend's wedding a week earlier. He was a nice boy and he worked at his family's bakery, the Progress Street Bakery, down near the river. Pauline was so taken with Stanley that she couldn't help thinking ahead. But she kept it to herself and for that day, she was helping her sister.

"Maggie, here is a nice gown. Try this on."

The saleswoman said she could take in only one dress at a time, as the fitting room was not large enough to accommodate more than one bridal gown. Maggie took the satin one and tried it on. She had trouble doing up the buttons. She called Pauline to come in to help her. The saleswoman pulled the curtain aside and offered to do up the tiny satin covered buttons for Maggie, so Pauline just stayed outside the fitting room.

Maggie came out of the the small room and twirled around. "Paulie, what do you think?"

"It's kind of plain, but I do like it. It's got so many buttons. How much is it?" Pauline asked.

"Thirty dollars," said the saleswoman. "And you'll want a veil too."

"And how much is a veil?" asked Maggie, dreading the answer. Thirty dollars was a month's wages as it was.

"It depends on what you want. They range from five to fifty dollars. Did you want a long length or a short length? Did you want lace? Or net? Or … I suggest something fancy, since the gown is so plain."

Maggie felt a little offended, but didn't let on. "Let me see what you have," she replied. She and Pauline looked them over, and looked at the prices. "We'll come back when my boyfriend and I set a date," she replied. Maggie took off the gown, and she and Pauline left the store.

"My, my, what an expense," said Pauline considering that that the each earned only about seventy-five cents a day.. "How are you going to get that much money, sis?"

"I'll save, that's how. If I put away a dollar a week, I should have enough to buy one in say, fifty years from now," she joked.

"Seriously, Maggie. If you did put away a dollar a week, or a dollar every two weeks, you could have enough money in say … thirty-five weeks, or seventy weeks. Oh, that's a

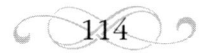

year or a year and a half. That's a long way off. If you want a June wedding, I'll help you out. I'll give you fifty cents out of my pay. I'd give you more, but I give Mama the same amount as you do … all my pay except except six dollars for myself. Maybe if we talk to Mama, she will help too, if she can."

"There is something else to think about. What if they don't have the gown when we go to buy it? Right now the gown and the veil would cost $35. The price might even go up."

The sisters walked the rest of the way home in silence, each wrapped-up in her own thoughts about hard times and the price of a wedding gown.

Their heads were down and their faces reflected the serious thoughts on their minds as they entered the house.

"Figlia mia, (my daughter) what's the matter? You look like your best friend died. What happened?" asked Mama.

Maggie and Pauline told Mama the problem.

"Of course I'll help. *Tu si mia figlia, ti volgio bene.*" (After all, you're my daughter. I love you.) She got up from the table they were sitting at and hugged Maggie. "How much is it? *Quanto costa?*"

"Mama, it is a lot of money! Thirty-five dollars for the gown and the veil.

"When you getting married, my daughter?"

"I don't know, Mama. Dave and I haven't talked about when. He just got hired at Conroy's. We have to talk about it."

"When you decide, let me know. I buy the gown for you. But my daughter, Dave has to talk to Papa first."

"Okay, Mama, he will."

115

Chapter 20
March 17-20, 1936:
The Pittsburgh Flood

⟨⟩

*Q*flood came to Pittsburgh. Many of the city's businesses, already struggling through hard times, suffered huge losses, and the Progress Street Bakery was among them.

When Stanley, who was now officially Pauline's boyfriend, told Pauline of his family's bakery disaster, she relayed the story to Maggie. One part of the story struck a funny cord in Maggie and she couldn't wait to tell Dave.

As the two strolled the narrow streets of the North Side on their way Islays one evening, to get skyscraper ice cream cones, Maggie could hardly control her laughter as she relayed this particular flood incident to Dave.

"Stanley had put the bread in to rise early in the morning at the bakery and then left to go back home. He was going to get his breakfast and go back again with his father, but then the river rose and they couldn't get back to the bakery because of the flood."

"Where is their bakery?" asked Dave.

"It's on Progress Street, near the river? Well, when they did get into the bakery they found all the loaves had risen alright—risen to the ceiling and stuck there! Can you just picture it, Dave?" Maggie started laughing again. "I know I shouldn't laugh, but I can't help it. It's so funny, if you can just picture it, but I guess it isn't so funny if it happened to you. I guess it cost them a pile of money and a lot of work."

Dave just smiled.

It was often this way with them. Maggie was talkative and laughed easily and Dave was quiet and more serious. Partly, it was his nature but he was also often tongue-tied in Maggie's presence. He couldn't think of anyone or anything but Maggie. There were other girls who tried to flirt with him. But he had no interest in them. Maggie was his love and she was special.

Sometimes when he was too quiet, Maggie would laugh and say, "What's the matter, Dave—cat got your tongue?"

The Iron Deer in the Park
April 1937

It was Saturday. Dave was going to see Maggie. He gave his hair a quick swipe with the comb—he always had that stubborn strand that fell over his forehead—and jammed the comb into his back pocket. He sprinted the short distance to Maggie's house. She was standing outside.

Dave reached for her hand. "Let's go, honey," Dave said. "Let's walk to the lake."

The couple walked hand in hand through the North Side streets. It was quite a walk to the park – to Lake Elizabeth – but they were full of energy.

Dave held Maggie's hand as they walked past the shops.

He wanted to ask her *again* to marry him, as it had been a full year since he last asked her. In his pocket was the signet ring from the Corps and that would have to do as a gift for now.

"You're too quiet, my Gypsy," said Maggie. "Speak to me, or did you forget I was here!"

He looked at her. "Don't be sore. How could I forget my sweetie walking right beside me." He took her hand. "I never thought I'd ever miss the old 'Burgh, but I did."

Nothing had changed. The same old men were hanging around the same old barber shop; it was the same people, the same stores. They walked past West Park and past the hospital, the post office, and the library. They stopped in front of the Buhl Planetarium.

"You want to look at the stars with me tomorrow night, Maggie?"

"You know I do, Gypsy, but not too late. I've got to be at work Monday at 7 A.M."

They arrived at the lake. "This lake is so big. There's the peanut man with hot peanuts. They smell good." Maggie twirled around with delight, like a small child. She bought a bag of peanuts. "Here, old man," she said to Dave. "Have some peanuts."

"I'm not interested in peanuts right now, dear, just you. Save the peanuts for later."

They walked around the lake to where the iron deer stood. Some little kids were playing on it. They sat down on the park bench and watched the kids play for a while.

"Well, David, we're here. Did you say you had something to show me? The deer, dear?" She laughed. She was happy.

He took out the ring.

She broke out into such a smile!

"Oh, David! But what kind of a ring is this? It's so odd looking."

The iron deer was there, steadfast, solid, ears perked up to all sound, eyes large, wide open, alert. The iron deer had been standing in the park next to Lake Elizabeth for as long as Dave could remember. It was a romantic spot, this deer standing in the grass under the trees. It was a good place to take a girl if you wanted her to set the date. The idea both frightened and excited him. It was all he thought of while had been away in the CCC. And now that he was working—to be with Maggie, to love her, to hold her, to have kids with her—it was all he wanted.

Maggie had said in her letters that there was talk of a second world war. Well, no war yet, so far. So, first things first. Ask Maggie to set a date, then talk to her folks.

He was worried about Maggie. He knew she loved him, but it seemed as if she didn't want to get married any too soon. She kept putting it off; probably because of money— or lack of it. And she did help her family out with money. After all, the country was in a serious depression, and work was hard to find.

Dave had gone from the red room to the shipping department at Conroy's, earning a small raise. It was great that Maggie worked there, as they sometimes had lunch together. Most of the time, however, she ate lunch with Nita and Pauline.

Nita silvered mirrors, mixing the formula and pouring the liquid silver onto the glass to form a mirror—

what a job! Maggie lifted the mirrors off one conveyer belt and placed them onto another. Pauline worked in the silvering room too, making sure the glass was clean and dry prior to silvering. The glass needed to be washed and very clean or the silver wouldn't adhere.

Eventually, the fact that the three sisters worked together cost Maggie her job when someone complained to one of the bosses that three people from one family were working for the company,.

Well, if Conroy & Prugh Glass let him go, there was always Fort Pitt Bedding down in Manchester, on Reedsdale Street, or was it Beaver Avenue? Oh well. Phil, Maggie's brother, worked at Isaly's. He could try there too, but he really wouldn't be good waiting on people. He was too shy and never knew what to say, unlike Phil, who was outgoing and always had a funny story to tell.

Dave liked Phil. Phil always made him feel comfortable and was always glad to see him, but then they were the same age—buddies almost.

On that particular night, Maggie was there with him all the while these thoughts were running through his head. He wished he could express some of them to her. He knew he did better at writing letters than talking. He could not always put his thoughts into words. But he knew he had to speak on that night.

"Maggie" he began,, "you said you would marry me. When? Can we set a date now?"

"Dave, yes. But tell me about this ring you gave me. What is it?"

Dave was not paying attention to what she asked; he had

his mind on marriage and the date. He knew she was chattering, but ignored her question about the ring.

"Dave, what about the ring?"

"It's a ring from the CCC. I got it while I was in camp. I thought you would like it."

"Dave, yes, it's odd, but nice. Here, take it and put it on my finger."

He turned her to face him. "Maggie, will you marry me, or do I have to get down on my knees to get a definite answer? Just say yes."

"Why, David, how sweet, darling. Yes, I will marry you, sweetheart, and no, you don't have to get down on your knees. Just don't go away again."

She held out her hand and he slid the ring onto her finger next to the one he had given her over two years earlier.

"Let's set a date now, Maggie."

"You have to talk to my papa first."

"Talk to your papa first!"

"Yes, David."

Dave felt daunted *—Talk to Maggie's father—about marriage!* Maggie's father seemed to Dave to be a formidable man. It would be hard for him to do this.

Time passed, Dave had still not gotten the courage to talk to Maggie's father but he continued working at Conroy & Prugh until he landed a better paying job at Fort Pitt Bedding, making seats for airplanes. He worked hard, saving as much as he could. Maggie worked too, of course, giving most of her pay to her parents. In their family, all the children gave nearly their whole pay to the family. Even though Maggie kept little for herself, she did manage to save for her wedding. The money went into her savings account at Workingman's Bank on East Ohio Street,

Chapter 21
A Wedding Ring

*D*ave wanted to buy Maggie a wedding band, so they went shopping together to look for one.

"How about this one?" Dave pointed to a large diamond ring in the pawn shop window. He was teasing her now.

"Not for me, David. If you really care for me, you wouldn't even think of buying it here. She walked away from the window and started down the street, pretending to be offended.

As they walked past Murphy's Five and Dime, Dave stopped and pulled her into the doorway. He went over to the bubble gum machine.

"How about it, Maggie, there's one for you," he said, pointing to the rhinestone ring inside the glass ball.

"David, the next thing you are going to tell me is maybe we can find a ring in a Cracker Jack box." They started walking.

"There's the jewelry store," Dave said. He had been working a little over a year and had enough saved up to buy her a decent wedding ring.

Maggie looked in the window. "David, look. It's so pretty." She indicated a yellow-gold ring.

"Yes, sweetheart, but I'm not a millionaire!" he said after seeing the price tag.

"Let's go in and see what else they have."

They entered the jewelry shop.

Just by looking at the couple, the clerk thought he knew what they wanted to see. He had seen hundreds of young couples, deeply in love and he had noticed the large ruby on Maggie's finger. Then reconsidering, he thought perhaps the classic empire setting was the girl's mother's ring.

"What can I do for you?" he inquired politely with an engaging smile.

"Er, a..." Dave stammered. It wasn't every day he was prepared to buy a wedding ring.

"We, ah... we'd like to see some wedding rings," he finally got out.

"Yes," added Maggie. "not too large."

The man got out a tray of beauties, which were displayed on black velvet.

Maggie tried on several and ended with the first one she had put on. It was fourteen karat gold. She felt like a princess. She was wearing the ruby ring her Godmother had given her for her Confirmation when she was twelve years old. She had left the other rings Dave had given her at home. She was wearing her old brown coat with the fake fur around the collar and her long dangling earrings with the pale blue diamond-like stones and matching necklace. Also for this special occasion, she wore a rhinestone clip in her hair and her new hat. She certainly looked elegant and stylish.

David, on the other hand, was his same boyish self, although perhaps a bit older now and appearing so since his stint of more than a year in the Corps and another year gone fast at Conroy & Prugh Glass Company. The past three years had added musculature and fresh vitality to his appearance. In his first year in the CCC, he had gained twenty pounds and put it into shear muscle by hard work in the forest. This past year, working first at Conroy & Prugh and then at Fort Pitt Bedding, gave him self-esteem, a look of maturity, and a little money in his pocket. And of course, he was in love with the classiest and certainly the most beautiful girl in the world. He looked at her fondly and with a certain possessiveness as she stood beside him in this fine jewelry store.

"David, what do you think about this one, dear? Do you like it?"

"Whatever you want, honey."

"David, please, do you like it?" she asked again.

"Yes, it's just right. Try it on."

Margaret slid the ring over the fourth finger of her left hand. The fit was perfect.

"It fits, David! Let's take it."

David proudly paid cash for the ring. The old jeweler was impressed. He usually got requests for credit.

"Would you be interested in seeing a wedding band for yourself, sir?" he offered.

"Thanks," they said in unison. "Not yet."

They left the store laughing. Dave held the velvet box in his pocket and Margaret had the ring on her left hand.

"David, I'm going to give you back the ring."

His heart lurched. "Honey, what is it, why?"

"David, you must do it properly, you know … ask Papa for his permission for my hand in marriage. That's the only way, or my papa will be angry."

"Okay. You had me scared for a minute. I thought you had changed your mind."

"David, let's go to the movies. There is a good movie playing. You can talk to Papa tomorrow. Sunday is a good day to talk to him."

The very next day, David went to Maggie's house and asked to talk with Mr.Rossi.

"Mr. Rossi," he began, "I have a good job. I care very much about your daughter Margaret. I want to marry her."

Mr. Rossi, who had gotten to know David by that time, liked him and trusted him. So he grinned. slapped David on the back, and shook his hand.

"You take good care of my daughter, no? I see you love a' her, eh? And when you gonna' get a' marry?"

"Hey, Mama, what you t'ink," Sam Rossi called out to his wife.

"This a fine young man wanta marry our Migalena. I say yes."

"Yes, Dave." Mrs. Rossi put her arms around David and gave him a great big hug.

Maggie was not far behind. She came into the room with all her sisters behind her. They were all excited, because they knew what was going on. Everyone was talking at once.

"David and I want to get married on June second," Maggie said above the noise.

"It has to be on a Saturday, Migalena," said Papa.

Anna ran to look at the calendar hanging on the back wall of the kitchen. She ran back with her information.

"June second is on a Saturday!"

"Then that's it," said Mr. Rossi.

"Now everybody, it is our wedding." But no one heard Maggie.

Nita, Pauline, Susie and Mary offered their congratulations with hugs and kisses. Susan came in.

They were all happy for Maggie and Dave but Susie had special feelings about the announcement. Maggie and Susie would often confide in each other at bedtime each night. Many of their talks had centered around their innermost wishes and dreams and what it would be like to be married to the one you loved.

"Susan, David and I want you and Phillip to be in our wedding."

"Did I hear my name?" Phil chimed in. "What wedding? Who's getting married?"

"As if you didn't know!"

Phil put his arms around his favorite sister and then held out his hand to Dave. "Congratulations, old man. When's the fatal day?"

"June second, I think." He looked at Maggie.

Let's get out of here, his eyes seemed to say.

"Dave and I are going outside to sit on the steps for a while," Maggie announced. They retreated from the din and clamor to the peace of outdoors, grabbing their coats as they went. It felt oh so good to get some fresh, cold air and privacy.

"What a family," Dave said.

"They're as excited as we are," said Maggie. But now we have to see the priest about the church, Dave."

"Let's go tell my mother,"

"Oh yes. We have to tell her right away," said Maggie.

They both got up from the cold front steps and went down the street to Dave's house.

But once inside, Mrs. Bell is nowhere to be found.

"It looks like she's gone out," said Dave.

The two sat down at the kitchen table to wait.

"You look different tonight, Maggie."

"I'm happy."

He laughed and pulled his chair sideways to get closer to her.

"I'm glad," he said. Then he did a daring thing—he ran his finger up the side of her leg. She pushed his hand away. He laughed and his eyes crinkled. "Why, don't you like it?"

"That's none of your business," she said loudly.

He tried it again and this time she slapped his hand and exclaimed with meaning, "You don't have a license for that!" and stood up. "I'm leaving." She put on her coat and walked out the door.

As she walked toward home, her thoughts flowed unhindered. She did like it. It made things happen inside her, made her feel tingly and warm in certain places, forbidden places. She didn't want anything to happen yet. If he really loved her, he could wait. They would be married soon enough.

Chapter 22
The Confession

Maggie entered the Church and genuflected, making the sign of the cross. There were a few people there, praying. It was quiet. Maggie went into the pew and knelt down. "Dear God, please help me make a good confession. I don't know if I sinned or not. These feelings I get when he touches me —I never felt like this before! Is it a sin to have these kinds of feelings?" She got up and stepped to the side of the church and into the confessional where the priest was seated.

"Father, forgive me, for I have sinned. It is one month since my last confession. I think I might need your help with my confession. I'm not sure if I sinned or not."

"What is it, my child?"

"Well this boy, I mean this man I know—well, we're getting married in June—he touched my leg."

"He touched your leg?"

"Yes, he ran his hand up my leg, my lower leg—below my knee."

"And then what happened?"

"I got this feeling."

"Did you do anything?"

"No. But then he started kissing my fingers, one by one."

"Did you do anything else? Did you kiss him? Did he kiss you?"

"No, Father, you see, we were sitting at the kitchen table, and I was talking and he just reached over and ran his hand up my leg , and then he began kissing my fingers, and I got up and opened the kitchen door and left."

"If you didn't do anything, child, this is not a sin."

"But these feelings I get, Father, when he touches me, aren't they sinful?"

"No, because you didn't act on those feelings. Tell me, do you love this man?"

"Yes, but it's hard to be sure, Father. I think so but I wish I was more certain. I mean I want to marry him but sometimes I'm confused."

"Then pray to the Lord for guidance, my dear, and God Bless you."

Chapter 23

The Church

Saint Mary's at Lockhart and Nash Streets was a classic Roman Catholic Church in that it was constructed in the shape of a cross with a long aisle down the middle between the pews, and a chapel on either side, forming the arms of the cross. The ceiling was made like a ship, ready to sail its parishioners right into heaven. The outside of the building was red brick, with three gothic front doorways trimmed in stone.

In 1937, Mass was still said in Latin, and the priest faced the crucifix, with his back to the parishoners. There was a communion railing, where people knelt to receive the host.

This was the church where Maggie had dreamed of coming down the aisle. She would be in all white, on the arm of her papa, walking past friends and relatives, to be met by her Dave at the foot of the altar where they would recite the holy marriage vows, promising to love and cherish each other until death parted them.

Dave kept his promise to Maggie and had recently been baptized and confirmed at Saint Mary's, entering into the Roman Catholic faith, so that the two could be married in the church.

A Wedding

It was time. Saturday, June 2, 1937, Saint Mary's Church on the North Side of Pittsburgh. The bride, her father, and her attendants were waiting in the rear of the church with nervous anticipation.

Maggie had slept well and woke up feeling refreshed and happy.

Before church that morning, Pauline was helping sixteen-year-old Susan get ready. She slipped on her pale pink chiffon ankle-length gown with a taffeta underskirt. Pauline helped Susan zip up the back.

"Phillip, you hurry now. Don't take your good old time like you always do," she yelled.

Phillip was grinning and trying to think up some mischief, but he couldn't think of anything just now. He had a special fondness for his sister Maggie, who was one year older. He loved teasing her and getting her mad as he had done the night before. But this time it had backfired on him.

Phil had been taunting Maggie about the honeymoon. "Hey, sis," he said, rolling his eyes, "whatcha gonna do on your honeymoon, honey?" At that, Maggie ran after him, chasing him up the stairs with a sharp pointed pencil. He didn't quite make it up the second flight of stairs when she caught up with him and stabbed him in his arm. But the pencil point broke off in his skin and he almost passed out when he saw it. When Maggie realized what she had done, she was immediately repentant and grabbed him and kissed him practically to death.

Now he was fully recovered from last night's ordeal and

standing here in the side aisle at the front of the church with his brother-in-law to be, David, who was pacing back and forth, saying he needed a cigarette.

Sue and Teenie, in the rear of the church with Maggie, saw that the flower girl, little Mary Popovich was making a face. She looked pretty in her white dress, long white stockings, and white Mary-Jane shoes. But the shoes were new and and they were pinching her. Besides that, she was cranky and sleepy, because her mom woke her up so early. Maggie's nephew, Sammy, the ring bearer, was having a shy spell and did not want to go up the aisle with the ring pillow. He got scared seeing all the people who would be looking at him. So, Jimmy, the son of one of Mrs. Rossi's friends, was told to carry the wedding pillow.

Ernie Gruber was busy ushering the family and guests. Dave could see his mother making her way down the aisle on Ernie's arm. She looked happy. Dave's sister Mary, her husband, Mike, and Millie were already in their seats.

Dave's brothers and their families were seated with the rest of the Bell family. He would have asked his brothers to be in the wedding party but they couldn't participate because they weren't Catholic.

Maggie's only married sister, Angelina, and her husband, Jim, and his family were there too. And of course, Maggie's Mama was in the first row beaming and looking lovely and proud.

There was a sudden hush as the organist began the entrance hymn. The bridesmaids stopped fussing with their gowns, shot quick glances at each other, straightened up, and began the slow procession down the aisle.. The music resounded powerfully as they walked, followed by the tiny flower girl and the replacement ring-bearer.

Maggie and her father waited in the back. She was beautiful in her simple satin gown and veil, holding her bouquet of white roses and baby's breath, not looking nearly as nervous as she felt. When the organist signaled the bride's entrance, Papa took Maggie's arm, and they started up the aisle.

Maggie wore a solemn expression and kept her eyes on the priest. She didn't want to look at Dave until the last minute; she was afraid she would burst out laughing—she was so happy. Finally, they reached the front, where her papa gave her to Dave. At that moment, when Maggie looked at her beaming groom, she smiled broadly and was so taken with him that she nearly tripped going up the three steps to the altar. The priest cleared his throat and Maggie and Dave looked forward.

"Dearly beloved, we are gathered here today to join together this man and this woman in the bonds of Holy Matrimony." The ceremony began with the priest's words.

After the opening prayers, said entirely in Latin, the priest stepped up to the podium to do the readings. He read passages from 1 Corinthians 13: 4-13. Verses 4 and 5: *Love is patient; love is kind. Love is not jealous, it does not put on airs, it is not snobbish. Love is never rude, it is not self-seeking, it is not prone to anger; neither does it brood over injuries.* Verse 6: *Love does not rejoice in what is wrong, but rejoices with the truth.* Verse 7: *There is no limit to love's forbearance, to its trust, its hope, its power to endure.* Verse 8: *Love never fails. Prophecies will cease, tongues will be silent, knowledge will pass away.* Verse 11: *When I was a child, I used to talk like a child, reason like a child. When I became a man I put childish ways aside.* Verse 12: *Now we see indistinctly, as in a mirror; then we shall see face to face.* Verse 13: *There are in the end three things that last: faith, hope, and love, and the greatest of these is love.*

When it was time for the recitation of the vows, the priest came over to the couple, and standing before them, asked, "Do you, David Dale, take this woman, Margaret Frances, to be your lawful wedded wife, to love, and to cherish until death do you part

"Yes, I do," was the reply.

"And do you, Margaret Frances, take David Dale to be your lawful wedded husband, to love, honor, and cherish until death do you part?"

"Yes, I will," Maggie said softly.

"Place the ring on her finger."

Then, after blessing the ring, the priest said, "I now pronounce you man and wife."

The sacred Mass continued with holy communion and the final blessings. Then the ceremony was over and the organ resounded with the recessional hymn.

Smiles and tears greeted the newly wedded couple as they walked, arm in arm, down the aisle. Once in the back of the church, in the vestibule, David and Maggie kissed their first kiss as husband and wife. Following the traditional receiving line, Maggie and Dave came out of the church to a hail of rice and cheers.

Papa's old Chrysler was all decorated with paper posies and streamers, and someone had tacked a "JUST

MARRIED" sign on the rear of the car.

Dave and Maggie got in the back seat and Phillip got in the front to drive them to Evans Studio for the wedding portraits.

Dave was quiet, as usual. But it was clear that he was happy. After all the waiting, he was finally married to his love. Both Dave and Maggie were looking forward to going to Washington, D.C. for their honeymoon.

Back home, after the studio pictures were taken, they all sat down for the wedding feast that Mr. and Mrs. Rossi and the family had prepared. There was a three-tiered, bakery-made wedding cake decorated with white roses displayed on a separate table for all to admire. There was the traditional wedding soup, breaded chicken, vegetables, salads, and pastas. There were also stuffed artichokes, one of Mama's specialties.

Someone had brought Torrone. And of course, there was Papa's homemade port and his special dandelion wine. There was anisette for the ladies, as Mama had requested. And Papa had made a piquant peach wine for this very special occasion. He also provided homemade root beer for the children.

The Christi family, friends of the Rossi's, had given a gift of pink and green anisette just for the toast, as everything was done in pinks and greens. There were delicious Italian cookies and ices, and white and pink pyramids of sugar bon bons that Maggie had ordered.

Mr. Napoli came in to play the accordion. Mr. Indovina, who owned a grocery store in Shadyside, and to whom Papa sold eggs, was also there to join the festivities.

After the meal and joyous hours of dancing, Margaret tossed the wedding bouquet and quietly disappeared upstairs to change into her blue traveling suit and white blouse. Her luggage was already packed for the honeymoon trip.

Phil was waiting outside to take them to the train station.

"Don't honk the horn this time, Phil," Maggie and Dave said in unison.

They were on their way to Washington, D.C. for the best time of their lives. They had no worries, no cares—only the future awaited them—a future filled with love.

The announcement in the newspaper read, *On June 2, 1937, at St. Mary's Church, North Side, Margaret Rossi was married to David Bell. The bride wore a full-length gown of white satin with a train of several feet. Her long veil cascaded down her back with a crown of tiny white flowers on her hair. In her arms she carried a bouquet of white roses and baby's breath with satin streamers.*

The wedding reception was held at the home of the bride's parents. Photography was done by Evans Studio. The couple honeymooned in Washington, D.C.

Part Two

Two years and one child later . . .

The Talk

The day was overcast and dreary. Maggie walked with her head down. She pushed the green wicker baby buggy slowly. The baby was cranky and seemed extra heavy today when she put her into the buggy, tucking the white frilly cloth snugly around her.

I hope she falls asleep by the time we get to Mama's house, she thought. *I need to talk to her about this. It is really bothering me.*

Maggie was so deep in thought as she walked that she didn't even notice when she got to the brick pavement which she usually avoided. The young mother walked down Madison Avenue, crossing Vista Street, where Mrs. Stanko lived. It was hard do steer the buggy over the uneven, chipped, red bricks. But Maggie hardly noticed. David was laid-off from work again and money was scarce. *It's a good thing Mama taught me to bake bread. It's a good thing I saved some money too,* she thought. *It's so discouraging, every time I save fifty dollars, he gets laid off. Maybe something good will happen today."*

David was out at that moment, looking for work. Most likely he would also stop at his mother's to visit.

As Maggie pushed the buggy around the corner to Lovett Way, she thought of the time she first met Dave. It seemed so long ago—five years—a lifetime. She was happy and carefree then. She had a job, money—she smiled to herself—*if you could call twenty-five cents an hour money.*

Her take-home pay was only eleven dollars a week, but at least she had no bills to pay. Maggie had never minded giving her mother the lion's share of her pay. She could do what she wanted with what was left and it was enough. Those days were gone forever. Maggie was a mother now and she loved her little Dolly. But she was pregnant again, and really did not know where their next dollar was coming from. If Dave did not get work soon, she didn't know what they would do. Why was life so hard?

Now she passed 'Old Granny's' house. He was probably settled in another place by now. It was years since the since little Frank Madden's drowning death. She mused, *I guess Old Granny thought he was indirectly responsible, since he was the one who lent the rowboat that had capsized.*

It's funny how people think—how they let things like that affect them, even though they aren't directly responsible. Well, I guess guilt eats us all up, in some way. Just like me, she thought.

She passed the narrow side alley that led to Dave's mother's house. And there was her own mother's house. She glanced up quickly at the place: white frame with green trim. Home—eight twenty-five Lovett Way. Three stories, three steps up to the doorway. Three steps up to her beloved, cheerful mother. Back home at last, where comfort awaited her.

It is tradition in all Italian families when they great each other to embrace and kiss. And the Rossi family, was no exception. In fact, the love here in this wholesome, close-knit Italian-Catholic family flowed and flowered in the parents and children.

Maggi stopped in front of the house and put the brake on the buggy. She lifted her baby out, went up the three steps to the door, opened it and went into the main room of the house—the kitchen.

"Hi, Mama," she smiled, "I'm here with my cranky baby."

Mrs. Rossi wiped her hands on her apron and came over to Maggie, encircling both mother and baby in her arms. After kissing Maggie on the cheek, she took the baby Dolly in her arms.

"*Mama mia, tu si bella, bambina mia!*" she exclaimed in Italian. With a smile on her face, she looked at Maggie.

"What a funny baby," she kidded. "What did you do, pinch her?" She laughed. Maggie's mama was always smiling and happy. "Sit down," she said to Maggie in Italian. "*Mangiasta*? Did you eat? Are you hungry?"

"I'm not hungry, Mama, but I'll have some coffee."

Mama got the small white pan and filled it halfway with water and put in two spoonfuls of coffee.

"Mary ground the coffee beans this morning before she went to school," Mama said.

She got two large white cups from the sideboard and two spoons from the drawer. She went out to the icebox and got the can of evaporated milk.

Maggie watched as her mother moved around the large kitchen. "Mama, I need to talk to you. Sit down, please."

"Yes—si si, my daughter," said Mama. "as soon as I strain the coffee."

Maggie's mother poured the aromatic brown liquid through the strainer into a tall blue porcelain coffeepot. Setting this down on the white tablecloth, Mama sat opposite her daughter at the round table.

"Okay, *tu parle*, (you talk) I listen."

"Mama, I went to see Dr. Styber yesterday. He says I should go see a specialist at the hospital. I'm having some trouble inside, Mama, I'm bleeding again. He says I should have the baby by another way, Mama, not the regular way."

Maggie knew she would have a hard time explaining this. Mama did not always understand English words and terms, and Maggie did not know the Italian words for *cesarean section*. They were not even in the Italian-English word book that she had studied at night school.

Dr. Styber, their family doctor, had said that she might need to have a cesarean section, but this would be decided by the other doctor, the specialist, or obstetrician.

"Mama, he says I should go to another doctor, a specialist. He says maybe I will need an operation in order to have the baby. Do you understand, Mama? *Capice*? At the hospital … Allegheny General, Mama."

Mama didn't quite understand. "You maybe bump yourself, Migalina *mia*. Rest. Take care of yourself. Dr. Styber is a good doctor, listen to him and rest."

Though she tried to calm her daughter, Maggie's mama was worried. Her Migalina was so young—twenty-three—to have this trouble. She, Francesca, was born in Sicily, *cincque-quattor anni* (fifty-four years ago) and was strong and healthy. She had a few of her babies at home with only a mid-wife, and the next day she was up washing clothes and cooking.

Maggie's mother wished her own mama was here to give advice. She always knew what to do. This was bad, this bleeding; it was not right. She had lost a few babies herself. It should not happen to her own daughter. She would pray. The good God, *Jesú,* and the *Bieda Madré* would help. And Sunday she would light a candle. One had to have faith.

"Well, Mama, what do you say?" asked Maggie.

"You go see this *specialé dotoré,* and tell me what he say. Angelina can go with you. Then we see what he thinks."

Since this was Monday, washday, Mama had soup cooking. She always made soup on washday.

Mama dished out the hot soothing soup, and they ate in silence, each with their own thoughts of what they had just talked about. Little Dolly slept soundly through the visit.

Maggie would ask Angelina to go with her to see the doctor. If David wasn't yet working, he might go too. But she did not want to worry him needlessly.

Dr. Smith's office was in the hospital itself. It was very different from Dr. Styber's office, which was in his home— a red brick party-wall house with stone steps leading up to a vestibule. The doctor lived upstairs with his wife and children, and his office was on the first floor. It was on Lockhart Street, the same street as Saint Mary's Church, where Maggie and David were married almost two years earlier.

Patients entered Dr. Styber's front door and stepped into a dimly lit hall crowded with a heavy oak seat that had a tall mirrored back, a deer head crowned with antlers, a coat rack, and an umbrella stand. A stinging antiseptic smell pervaded the nostrils as patients sat in the living/waiting room in dark, hard-backed, chairs lined-up against glassed-in book cases, filled with dark, mysterious tomes.

Dr. Smith's office was sparsely furnished, brightly-lit, sterile, and devoid of all personal affects.

On the day of her visit to Dr. Smith, Maggie was examined first and then after a brief wait, she and Angelina had been called into his office for a consultatiion.

"Yes, a cesarean section might be the answer,' Dr. Smith explained, "but at this point, I don't know that it will be necessary. We will wait to make that decision. But if your bleeding doesn't subside, you will have to be admitted to the hospital for observation. In the meantime, I'm going to prescribe some pills for you and I want you to go home and rest—stay off your feet as much as possible, and find someone to take care of your little girl. Call me in a couple of days to let me know how you are doing. Make an appointment to come in a week from today."

The sisters left the office hardly knowing what to think. Dr. Smith certainly did not give any satisfaction as far as making them feel better about the situation. Maggie was a little anemic from the loss of blood, so Dr. Smith prescribed iron tablets.

"We'll stop at Watson's Drug Store and get the pills before we go home."

At home, Maggie told Mama what the doctor said.

"I take care of your little butterfly, your Dolly," Mama said. "Don't worry, I take care of her like she was you. Don't

worry. Leave her here with me right now. Angelina, you walk Maggie home and see she go to bed and rest. Tell Dave make some good soup. I send bread home with her. And take this chicken." She shooed them out the door. "It will make good soup."

Mama sat down at the table holding her little granddaughter.

Maggie was admitted to the hospital two weeks after her visit to Dr. Smith. She was bleeding heavily and though she wasn't yet in labor, she was full term.

When Dr. Smith was unable to slow the bleeding, he ordered the nurse to contact Maggie's husband. By the time Dave arrived at Allegheny General Hospital, he was told that Maggie had been taken into the delivery room.

"Mr. Bell," the nurse told him, "your wife is bleeding heavily—hemorrhaging—and you'll have to sign these papers indicating who should be saved—your wife or your child. I'm sorry. You might want to call your priest."

"I don't understand. What do you mean? Why do I have to make a choice? I want both of them. What are you talking about?"

"Your wife is hemorrhaging severely." explained the nurse. "We are giving her whole blood. Is there anyone else here from her family who can give blood?"

"You are the patient's sister?"

"Yes I am," said Nita.

" Your blood matches. Just follow me."

Nita followed the nurse into the small sterile room. "Just

lie down on this table."

"Take as much as you need. My sister, Pauline is giving blood too. I'm so worried about my sister. Is she going to be all right? Oh God this is terrible."

"Yes, your sister Pauline is behind that curtain over there, but we need more blood. Your sister, Maggie is doing as well as can be expected," the nurse said softly.

The nurse tried to reassure Nita, but she didn't have much hope. She had seen cases like this before. This was a case of placenta previa. The patient should have been closely monitored at the first sign of bleeding, which usually happened during the seventh or eighth months. In this case, Maggie was full term and had only just been admitted into the hospital. If the artery ruptured, she could die.

There should have been a C-section before this, the nurse thought.

"Nita, do you know anyone else who can give blood?"

"Yes, my sister Ange. I called her before I came in to the hospital."

Meanwhile, several miles away at Angelina's house in Shadyside, she was having trouble convincing her husband. "Jim,please take me to the hospital, please!"

"Ange, they don't need you; your sister Maggie will be fine. Women have babies every day."

"Jim, if you don't take me in the car, I will go myself ... if I have to walk."

"Okay, okay, we go."

Jim waited while the nurse tested Angelina for her blood type. She desperately wanted to give blood for her sister, but she did not have the right type. Disappointed and frightened, Angelina could only wait and pray with the rest of the family who had gathered in the waiting room.

It was tiny, this little microcosm of future fate, this microcosmic detail of dynamite, this carrier of ruination.

It floated, arbitrarily, merrily making its way, searching for a soft spot to implant itself.

It landed in the wrong spot.

It attached its twenty villi lower in the uterus than it ought, with portending danger to its host, and it grew, encircling the embryo that was to become a boy-child, the second born of Maggie and David.

He didn't have a chance, this boy-child. Fate saw to that.

When the doctor entered the room, his expression confirmed their worst fears. Dave could hear Maggie's mother and sisters sobbing as the physician approached him.

"Mr. Bell," he said quietly. "Neither your wife nor the baby made it. We did our best, but she lost too much blood and the baby—it was a baby boy— couldn't have survived. "I'm sorry."

The Coffee Pot

It is said that there are four stages of grief: shock, disbelief, anger, and finally acceptance. Everyone goes through these stages at their own pace, in their own way and time.

The kitchen was dark. The long rays of early morning light filtered over the table, the chairs, and the stove. It was spring outside this lonely kitchen. One window was open a few inches and you could hear the birds chirping and hear the few cars rumbling over the narrow cobblestone street.

Dave walked into the kitchen and automatically picked up the coffee pot and held it under the kitchen faucet.

The water gushed out filling the cold aluminum cylinder. Dave tossed it out, turned on the hot water, and refilled the coffee pot. Next, he went over to the cupboard and pulled down the red and black Eight O'Clock Coffee bag. He opened the drawer, picked out a measuring spoon, and carefully measured out four tablespoons of stale ground coffee. He glanced up at the calendar; the year was 1939, the month was May. He put the pot on the stove and turned on the gas, lighting the burner with a wooden matchstick.

He sat down. Loneliness filled his world now—stark and desolate. Dave was still dumbfounded. He knew what happened, but his mind would not accept it. He knew because he had seen her, his Maggie, lying still and cold in the casket. She was beautiful even in death. When he stared at her lying there, it seemed as if she did move—ever so slightly, but it was only his wish, his imagination. Someone had told him she was dead, someone gently laid a hand on his shoulder and walked him away from her and his dead infant son—his boy whom he would never know. The boy was lying there Maggie's arms. The baby was holding a satin ribbon flowing down from the mouth of a white dove.

The coffee was perking now, and the good smell invaded the kitchen. Dave sat quietly in the dark room. The darkness was soothing. It had only been two weeks after all, two weeks ago—or was it more? He shook his head—he still didn't believe it. But he felt it—he felt the absence of her warmth, her laughter, her embrace, and her light morning kisses.

What was he to do without her?

The next few years were a difficult adjustment. David moved about automatically doing what was expected—going to work, buying groceries, keeping the house clean. He had his mother move in with him. But little Dolly remained in the care of Maggie's parents. Everyone agreed it was best—Dave had to work. His Mother, now in her seventies, was too old to care for a one-year-old child. Besides, the last time Maggie spoke to her mother she had said, "Mama, take care of my baby, please, until I come home."

Maggie never came home, so Dolly stayed with her grandma, grandpa, aunts and uncles who loved and nurtured her, and watched her grow up. The big Rossi family was lively and their household was always full of people, good food, and plenty of fun.

Dave would visit Dolly often. He would take the tiny tot walking through the streets of the North Side, holding her small hand just as he had held Maggie's on their many walks. Though Dolly would have no memory of her mother, she would have remembrances of her young father dressed in his gray suit, wearing a fedora, looking down at her with great sadness.

When World War II broke out, Dave was inducted into the United States Army Corps of Engineers. He served in

Germany, France, and Egypt and even met the Queen of Egypt. While away, he wrote faithfully to his daughter, even sending her a picture of him on a camel.

When, after four years, he returned home safely from the war, his little daughter hardly recognized him. Dave had lost weight and some of his teeth. But he was still the same thoughtful man he had been with Maggie and he brought Dolly a pretty, gold locket, which she cherished.

Shortly after his return from the war, Dave's mother died. Dolly was thrilled when her father accepted her grandparents' invitation to live in their house.

Dave had his own tiny apartment on the second floor of the Rossi home and every day Dolly greeted him happily when he came home from work. She would take his lunch bucket and carry it upstairs for him and sit with her dad while he relaxed after a hard day at work.

When Maggie died, Dave had taken all of Maggie's clothes and belongings and packed them in her cedar chest. When he moved into the Rossi house, Dave brought the precious chest with him It was understandable when Dave told friends that he felt his whole life was over. But it indeed was not. Though he could never forget his Maggie, Dave was still a very young man.

After being home from the war a while, Dave began dating. One day he brought a special young woman home to meet his daughter and the Rossi family. Dave called his friend "Irish" and Dolly was impressed with the woman's beautiful black hair and smooth, lovely skin. Irish did her best to make a good impression and brought Dolly a bunny doll that had a smiling face with dimples.

Dolly was eleven years old when Dave and Irish married. In an effort to solidify their family, they took Dolly on their wedding trip to Geneva on the Lake—though Dolly had no idea she was on a honeymoon.

Since Dolly was always so happy living with her grandparents, it was decided that she would remain with them. Eventually Dave and his new wife had a son, David Dale, Jr. II and Dolly had a brother.

Dolly would frequently visit her father and his family and as she grew older, Dave would often take her up to the attic where he kept Maggie's cedar chest, still packed with her things. Though he told her little, Dave would show her Maggie's favorite handbags, jewelry, and some of her clothes. It was the only way he knew to give his daughter some small piece of the wonderful mother she had lost.

Years passed, the Bell children grew up and Dave grew old. Forty-five years had gone by since the day Maggie died. Though her father was always close to her, Dave never spoke about her mother, Maggie. And Dolly knew that he never visited her grave.

Dave had always worked hard, never earning more than minimum wage. He worked in a greenhouse, caring for commercially-grown flowers and delivering them. Because the greenhouse owners appreciated Dave's dedication, they allowed him a half acre to plant whatever he chose and they would give him the use of two tables in one of the greenhouses. He terraced the hilly half-acre and planted all kinds of vegetables. But in the greenhouse, Dave delighted in growing rare plants, like giant desert cacti, Night Blooming Cerus, miniature lace geraniums, and pepperomia plants. And he took great pleasure in sharing them with Dolly.

One day only a few years before Dave died, Dolly and her father were on their way to her brother's farm when they happened past the cemetery where Maggie was buried. In that instant, the two looked at each other and locked eyes. Suddenly, Dolly could feel an emotion between them that seemed to fill the car. It was as if father and daughter became one and communicated an understanding that needed no words.

The look in Dave's eyes told Dolly all she needed to know—that the pain of losing Maggie had been too great for him to put into words. That the memory of her was so alive and real that he couldn't bare to visit a mere grave site.

When Dave died in 1984, just twenty days after his sixty-eighth birthday, he left Dolly a wonderful legacy. Though he had never acquired wealth, he left no unpaid debts. Dolly's brother, David got their father's familiar, old van and Dolly received the best gift of all—the cedar chest filled not only with her mother's belongs but with the letters—love letters Dave had written Maggie from the CCC camp and even some that Maggie had written him in return. Not only did the letters communicate a wealth of detail about the love her parents felt for each other, but the fact that Dave had kept them sent a powerful message to his daughter.

Though Dolly's mother was taken from her and her father seemed unable to tell his daughter about Maggie, the letters seemed to come from heaven itself as a message of love for all generations.

The End

CCC Facts

From Tony Shively's book, ***The CCC Camps of Union County.***

Tea Springs Camp was established in May 1933. The original company consisted of two hundred enrollees, including fifteen local men. The company doctor was Adrian J. Delaney of the U.S. Navy.

The principal work area of Camp S-114 consisted of approximately thirty thousand acres of the Bald Eagle State Forest in Union, Centre, and Clinton Counties.

Work projects of the camp included road construction, forest stand improvement, blister rust control, telephone line construction, tree planting, and road and trail maintenance.

Camp S-114 also served as the CCC Sub-District 9 Headquarters. As a result of the flooding along the Susquehanna River in the spring of 1936, much of the historical data pertaining to the sub-district was either lost or destroyed. The Tea Springs Camp closed in the fall of 1935.

The expression, 'barring rock,' means using a crowbar to lift and lever the rocks from the road bed or earth.

According to Betty Simcox, the Tea Springs Camp was headquarters for a sub-district of eleven camps. James Koch was Chief Clerk of the sub-district. Some of the members were James Koch, Clarence Powers, Andy Salamon, Frank Wertz, Richard Miller, Jack DeLong, William Scaff, Sr. (Head Cook), Glenn Klobe, John Long, Tom Long, Charles DeHaas, Miles Frank, H. Rufus Frank, John Frank, James Brungard, Warren Witmyer, and Emory Bletz.

The CCC was run by the Department of Agriculture, the Forest Service, and the Department of the Army.

As per Leonard Parucha of McKeesport, formerly of the CCC, he was sworn in at the North Side Branch of the Pittsburgh Post Office.

According to a letter sent to the author from Leonard Parucha: "Basically the bridges that we built in the early years of the CCC were to get across small strams. We had no heavy equipment so most of the work was by hand. And we had no cement nor steel girders. All bridges were single span and the girders were long pine logsmade from trees that we cut down in the immediate area. Ofcourse, our small bridges were not that durable and most of them were washed out by the 1936 flood.

Footnotes:
1. P.14 Pigs Run – Now called Rialto Street.
2. P. 57 DYSLM – Do You Still Love Me?
3. P. 84 Joe Penner was a radio comedian.

Main source of information:
Letters written by David Dale Belin when he was in the CCC, from 1934 to 1935.
Letters written by Margaret Frances Racculia from 1934 to 1935.

Bibliography:
Salmond, John. The Civilian Conservation Corps., 1933-1942: A New Deal Case Study: pub. by Duke Univ., Durand, NC 1967

Shively, Tony. The CCC Camps of Union County (1933–1942): Life and Work in the Civilian
Conservation Corps. Union County Historical Society (Pub. 2002, copyright 2001).

Pennsylvania Profiles. Pennsylvania Magazine (July/Aug. 1998; p. 31).

Legacy of the CCC. Pennsylvania Magazine (March/April 2003; pp. 34-39).

To the CCC. Smithsonian Magazine (Dec. 1994; pp. 66-78).

Letters:
Robert Edgar; Lock Haven, PA
Jeannette Zimmerman; Lock Haven, PA
Leonard F. Parucha; Lock Haven, PA

Interviews:
Louis Mayer; Trafford, PA
James (Jim) M. Koch; Loganton, PA
Ruth and Bill Soo; Loganton, PA

Information:
Carnegie Library of Pittsburgh
Oakland Branch
Pennsylvania Room
Pittsburgh, PA 15213

National Archives Trust Fund_NNRC
700 Pennsylvania Ave. NW
Washington, DC 20408

National Personnel Records Center
Civilian Personnel Records
111 Winnebago Street
St. Louis, MO 63118

National Association of the CCC Alumni
NACCCA Journal
PO Box 16429
St. Louis, MO 63125-0429
(Located at 16 Hancock Ave., Jefferson Barracks)

Online:
NARA Research Room (National Archives & Records Administration)

Dave and Maggie at the farm.

Maggie at about the time of her engagement, wearing the blue "diamond" earings and fur piece.

Dave and David Belin, 1937, at camp.

The Civilian Conservation Corp Camp at Loganton, Pennsylvania.

The CCC camp in the winter of 1934.

The one-time Rossi family home on Lovett Way as it appears today.

Dave's sister, Millie Madden with her nephew, Charlie.

The iron deer in West Park.

Maggie's brother, Phil.

Maggie and Dave's wedding portrait.
June 2, 1937

Saint Mary's Church at
Lockhart and Nash.

*Maggie and Dave with their baby daughter, Margaret Frances,
whom they called Dolly, at the farm, October, 1938.*

The Rossi sisters with Dolly in front of Lake Elizabeth at West Park.
From left: Nita, Annie, Maggie, Dolly, Pauline, and Mary

Baby Dolly and her father, Dave at the farm.

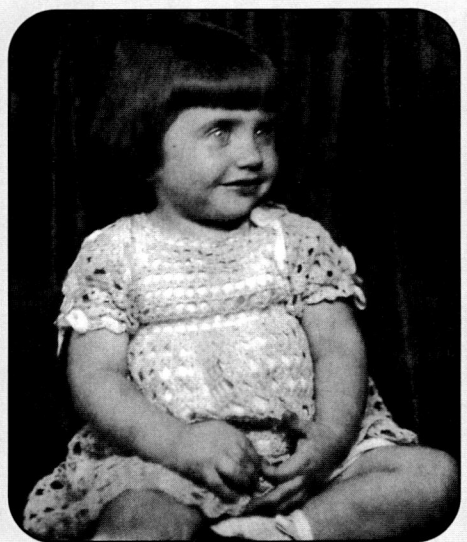

Dolly at age three.

*Dolly at age five, taken
at G.C. Murphy Five and
Ten on the North Side.*

Maggie's sister, Nita (far left) walks the picket line.

A reunion of CCC camp workers after the war.
Left to right: Mac, Dave, and Fergie.

Maggie's parents, Sam and Frances

Pittsburgh's Water Street, looking toward The Point, May, 1932.

Mama's Recipes

MAMA'S HOMEMADE BREAD

Makes 3 medium size loaves.

7-1/2 to 8-1/2 Cups sifted flour   1/4 Cup oil or
cooled, melted Crisco   1 Blessing
3 Cups warm water   2 tsp. Salt
2 packets dry yeast
Extra flour

Pile all of the flour in a large pot or bowl. Make a
depression in the middle. Add yeast, salt, 2-1/2 Cups
warm water, and oil. Slowly mix the flour into the
mixture. Mix with hands until all of the flour is not seen,
adding more flour or water as necessary.
Knead as with any bread, for about 10 minutes. Make a
Sign of the Cross over the dough. Let rise in a warm
place, for about two (2) hours, covered with a clean cloth
or dishtowel, until about double in size. Punch down and
shape into loaves. Place into lightly oiled pans. Let the
loaves rest for about an hour, covered. Preheat oven to
400 degrees. Put a pan of water in the bottom of the oven.
Bake the loaves for 35 minutes. When the loaves are
done, they will have a hollow sound when you rap them
with your knuckle. Take them out of the pans
immediately and place on a clean cloth. Do not cover.
Let cool. Enjoy!

STUFFED ARTICHOKES

4 artichokes
1/2 Cup vegetable or olive oil
2 cups Italian seasoned breadcrumbs
About 1/2 Cup Water
4-6 cloves garlic, minced
About 1/2 teaspoon Salt to taste
1/4 Cup Parmesan Cheese

Rinse artichokes, remove bottom leaves, the ones that are dark. Holding artichokes by the bottom, turn them upside down and pound them hard a few times on a countertop to open up the leaves. Cut off some of the bottom stem, about _ inch or so. Mix together the bread crumbs, garlic and oil, and cheese. Hold the individual leaves open and fill with the bread crumb mixture. After filling the artichokes, if they seem dry on top, add some of the 1/2 cup water to each. If you use a pressure cooker, use the meat rack and put the artichoke stems in the holes. Set the temperature at #15, with the bottom covered with water, 1 inch deep. Cook for 25 minutes, after the top jiggles, and turn down the heat to low. If you use a regular covered pot, set the artichokes in the pot so that they stand up by themselves and do not fall over. Fill the pot with 3 cups of water and take care the water does not evaporate, as they must cook slowly for about an hour, with a tightly covered lid. To eat, let them cool on a plate. Take off the leaves, one at a time. Place in your mouth, sliding the bread crumbs off with your teeth. Eat only the bottom part of the leaf, which is soft. Do not eat the tops of the leaves; discard them. The middle or core of the artichoke may be eaten also. The taste has to grow on you, but they are very good once you get used to the exotic taste.

FRIED ARTICHOKE SLICES

2 or 3 artichokes   Salt and/or pepper
2 eggs   Vegetable or olive oil
1/2 cup flour

Wash artichokes. Cut tops slightly. Slice artichoke in half from the top down. Slice again in quarters. Slice quarters, then slice each quarter again until you have several thin slices. Beat eggs and add salt and pepper to beaten eggs. Dip each slice into the egg and then into the flour. Put oil in frying pan and heat, add artichoke slices, and cook until golden in color. Enjoy!

WEDDING SOUP

1 small whole chicken   1/2 lb. ground beef
4 bullion cubes   2 tablespoons parsley
1 gallon water
Fresh spinach, cleaned and chopped.
1/2 small onion.
Dumplings, or pastina
1 clove garlic

Clean chicken and place into pot. Bring to a boil, skimming off any scum. Let chicken simmer for an hour. Remove chicken and let it cool. Add one tablespoon parsley, finely chopped onion, and bullion cubes to soup. Remove chicken from bones, chop, and add to soup. Add spinach. Make tiny meatballs from ground beef and remaining parsley, and add to soup. Simmer one-half hour. Add little dumplings, or cooked pastina.

M argaret Soboslay grew up in the Shadyside section of Pittsburgh, raised by her beloved grandparents. She graduated from Sacred Heart High School and attended Allegheny Community College and Carlow College. She is the mother of six daughters, eleven grandchildren, and one great grandchild. Now a retired medical transcriptionist from Health America and Keystone Rehabilitation Systems, she persues her interest in writing and in art.